Marie L. Erwin
1213 - 40th Avenue
Sacramento, Calif.
95822

D1443658

DESIGN
FOR FLOWER ARRANGERS

All Design Comes From Nature

DESIGN
FOR FLOWER ARRANGERS

by

DOROTHY W. RIESTER

DIAGRAMS BY THE AUTHOR

D. VAN NOSTRAND COMPANY, INC.
PRINCETON, NEW JERSEY
TORONTO   LONDON
NEW YORK

D. VAN NOSTRAND COMPANY, INC.
120 Alexander St., Princeton, New Jersey (*Principal office*)
257 Fourth Avenue, New York 10, New York

D. VAN NOSTRAND COMPANY, LTD.
358, Kensington High Street, London, W.14, England

D. VAN NOSTRAND COMPANY (Canada), LTD.
25 Hollinger Road, Toronto 16, Canada

———————

COPYRIGHT © 1959 BY
D. VAN NOSTRAND COMPANY, INC.

———————

Published simultaneously in Canada by
D. VAN NOSTRAND COMPANY (Canada), LTD.

———————

Library of Congress Catalogue Card No. 59-14620

———————

No reproduction in any form of this book, in whole or in part (except for brief quotation in critical articles or reviews), may be made without written authorization from the publishers.

PRINTED IN THE UNITED STATES OF AMERICA
BY LANCASTER PRESS, INC., LANCASTER, PA.

Foreword

Man's ability—one might even say compulsion—to design is one of the major traits which set him off from the other primates. By means of it he has refashioned large sections of the natural world to contribute to his basic needs of food, clothing, and shelter. But in addition he has from the earliest times sought something more through the arts of design: namely, the satisfaction of aesthetic needs.

Although the aesthetic aims and methods of visual design were intuitive and natural with early man, and to some extent will always remain so, in our advanced stage of civilization such activities cannot be left to develop naturally. Excellence in visual design now requires careful study of its principles and training in its practice. That is the reason for books such as this one; for in it may be found so much of the wisdom of the ages that generations of trial and error can be circumvented by its use.

Flower arranging is often considered to be one of the arts of design farthest removed from the so-called practical needs of everyday life. Yet it has a long history and in modern times has reached a stage of great refinement. He who really masters its principles, and succeeds at the same time in using it freely as a medium of individual expression, will have found the key to all the other arts of design. It can unlock for him the pleasures and profundities of music, of architecture, of painting, of poetry. In this sense, therefore, flower arranging has broad practical values.

By the same token, this book, though directed toward a specific art form, is in fact a basic text in the art of design in general. Its author exemplifies its principles in every part of her daily life. She has been active in the creative side of sculpture, ceramics, architecture, and industrial design. She has made her influence felt in her community through participation with others in promoting art museums, city planning and other efforts to improve the physical environment. Furthermore, she loves to teach. For these reasons this book cannot fail to enrich the lives of its readers.

Harris K. Prior, *Director*
The American Federation of Arts

v

Author's Preface

The Meaning of Design

This is primarily a book on design, as it concerns all the arts. Because of the great need for a thorough, contemporary text in flower arranging, I have used diagrams and modifying examples from this area. Substitute diagrams and examples from another art, and this will become a book on design for that art.

The final purpose of every artistic expression is to give insight to the deeper, hidden meanings of life. As Susanne Langer expresses it—, "to give form to feeling." Each artist will have his own intent, and every media will have its own characterizing limitations, but the ultimate aim and the basic design principles remain the same in all the arts.

We have become so accustomed to looking at and classifying separate art forms that we often fail to see their inner relationship and to realize that they are all ways of knowing the mysteries and wonder of life.

Art cannot be seen as a static form to be classified, nor can design be taught or thought about in such a way. Design is not an accomplished fact. It is not a formula to be memorized. Rather it is an activity, a doing. From the first selection and placing together of materials, we seek rhythmic relationships, transitions and interests. As we work, a unifying structure gradually emerges which is one and inseparable with the form. This we call the design. To achieve it, the structure, we cannot begin at the end with a predetermined design, but as in life, with each new work, we must begin at the beginning.

This book is about the process of designing and about the necessary controlling disciplines of intent, imagination, and knowledge.

Techniques, procedure, and general visual reaction can be taught as established facts, but this is only a small part of designing. Knowledge alone will not create a work of art. It must be guided by intent and imagination, and this process cannot be taught. For it is impossible to teach an idea, impossible to teach imagination or perception or sensitivity. However, these essentials of creative designing can be cultivated in another but only with his full consent and co-operation. Although it is impossible to teach anyone to be creative, it is possible to give insight and to inspire another to find the spark within himself.

For me the writing of this book has been a long, slow, sometimes anguished process because the nature of art is elusive and defies description. To give the merest glimpse of it has been most difficult. Words tend to sound authoritative and this automatically destroys the very idea they are meant to express, that is, that final authority lies not in words but ultimately in each one of us through our understanding and our work.

We are freed from the authority of words when the discipline of an art has been understood. Disciplines of design are necessary in that they train the eye to see more deeply and simply and clearly. They offer a starting place and limitations for us to push against. When we have mastered these disciplines, we are free to create.

No rule, no discipline is an end in itself. The end in every art is to make the form come to life and acquire meaning. Design is the vehicle; communication is the end.

DOROTHY W. RIESTER

Syracuse, New York
July, 1959

Contents

Chapter 1

Creative Approach to Design

Since I am a sensitive creature surrounded by a universe utterly out of scale with myself, I must, therefore, address it questioningly but trustfully, and it must reply to me in my own terms, in symbols and parables, that only gradually enlarge my childish perceptions. It is as if Substance said to Knowledge: My child, there is a great world for thee to conquer, but it is a vast, and ancient, and a recalcitrant world. It yields wonderful treasures to courage, when courage is guided by art and respects the limits set to it by nature. I should not have been so cruel as to give thee birth, if there had been nothing for thee to master; but having first prepared the field, I set in thy heart the love of adventure. *George Santayana*

In these lines Santayana touches upon the essential nature of art for art is a way of knowing, a way of relating ourselves to the world about us. Art is a humanly created symbol which helps us to see the unknown, and the invisible. As Paul Klee expresses it, "Art does not reproduce the visible; rather, it makes visible."

As an artist, I must approach the universe questioningly and trustfully. I must seek and experience it before I can create meaningful symbols on my own terms. When I design—that is when I organize my inner vision into visible coherent form—I must keep in sight this vision as I select, place, and relate each shape, color, and texture. Design is not a separate, externally applied structure but rather the very fiber of art. When we approach design with courage and sensitivity and a high sense of adventure, the world yields us wonderful treasures of experience.

WHAT IS DESIGN?

Design is the result of a spontaneous, intuitive impulse to find order. It is instinctive for us to find order and interest in our environment. Without thinking, we straighten a tie or rearrange the articles

I

on a table. And we are affected by a lack of design. We become bored with uninteresting surroundings, depressed by ugly conditions, confused by disorder. A crowded city street, a chaotic shopping center can make us physically ill. The need for order is not only aesthetic but physical as well.

To design is to bring orderly form out of chaos.

In All Arts the Same Principles

The materials, shapes and objects which the designer uses become visual symbols, as in speech, words and gestures are symbols of communication. To design is to place visual symbols in orderly, rhythmic patterns which the eye can readily follow and thereby find satisfaction and meaning.

Since the human eye as a seeing machine is basically the same in all of us, there are design relationships or principles which are universal. Plates 1 to 5 represent art forms from widely separated times and cultures, yet our eye easily follows the balancing rhythms of lines, textures, light and dark, of open and closed space in each of them. In these illustrations, we can also trace a basic formal similarity in the circular rhythm about a central symmetric axis.

Through this universal, timeless language of art, we cross personal and cultural barriers and thereby grow in understanding and appreciation. No great work of art—music, ballet or painting—can belong to one political party or nation. It is the common property of all mankind.

Throughout this book, which is a design text for flower arrangers, I frequently refer to other arts and illustrate design with examples from painting, sculpture and architecture, since each art acts as a stimulant to every other art and is related to it. In studying the illustrations, you will find the same basic principles of organization in each, although the final forms are different. You can see at a glance that one form is sculpture, another architecture, a third flower arrangement. Within each form, you can further distinguish cultures, historical periods and schools of influence. You can also recognize the personal technique and interests which make an artist's work uniquely his. However, while the principles remain the same, the form changes with time, use, media and the intent of each artist. Let us now consider form.

PLATE 1. Bronze Statue of Shiva from Tibet. A circular, basically symmetrical composition in which every texture and shape has been directed into an undulating rhythmic line. (Courtesy, American Museum of Natural History)

FORM

Form is the complete expression; it is important to differentiate between *form* and *shape*. Form is the sum total of every idea, skill, movement, texture, color and relationship which created it. For example, the human form is the total expression of its organic make-up, of inherited and acquired traits, physical posture and spiritual attitude. The form of a flower arrangement is also the sum of all that

PLATE 3. Basalt Pre-Columbian Head of Macaw. A bold dynamic movement around a straight central axis has been created by the placement of openings and by contrasting shapes and textures. (Courtesy, American Museum of Natural History)

PLATE 2. Hispano-Moresque Tapestry of Silk and Metal (XIII–XIV Century). Within a circle, symmetrically placed figures are abstracted into triangular and rectilinear shapes. These dynamically contrast in texture and value. (Courtesy, Cooper Union Museum)

has gone into it. It is the design relationship, plus the material, plus the space and light around it, plus the imagination and sensitivity of its creator.

Form can be seen and classified, but it cannot be experienced in the same way by everybody, for we see as individuals with different

PLATE 4. English Bow Porcelain Figure (XVIII Century). A composition of curving lines around the central axis of the figure. The distinguishing characteristics are the ues of curved lines only and the emphasis on textural detail. (Courtesy, Cleveland Museum of Art, Gift of Mrs. A. M. Luntz)

PLATE 5. "Mother and Child" by Jacques Lipchitz (XX Century). A symmetrical, curvilinear composition which derives its distinguishing power and form from the balancing of proportionate placements of semiabstracted round and angular shapes. (Courtesy, Cleveland Museum of Art)

backgrounds. Furthermore, our sensitivity varies. A feeling for form can be developed, but we will always have our own preferences and interpretations. Form is seen as a human experience, and like human beings, it is constantly subject to change.

SHAPE

Shape, on the other hand, can be geometrically defined and understood in the same way by everyone. An arrangement, described as triangular, square or spherical, will mean the same to each of us. *Shapes remain constant.* A rectangle drawn 5,000 years ago looks the same as a rectangle drawn today, but the drawing of a man made 5,000 years ago will not look like the drawing of a man of today. We recognize both as men but the form has changed.

The difference between an ancient Egyptian drawing of a man and a drawing of a twentieth-century man is distinguishable by much more than costume. The proportions, postures and emphasis on the part of the artist are different. In each drawing, we could find similar shapes but each would have its own expressive form. As designers, we work with shapes but our ultimate concern is form. *In form lies the life of the design.*

STYLE

Form changes with the taste of society, the climate of growth and the frame of reference. These influence the designer's choice of materials, colors, proportions and rhythms. The formal result is called *style*. A style may go on for centuries with little change, as it did in Egypt, or be subject to constant alteration, as in America today. An unchanging style becomes decadent when artists no longer create but blindly copy what has gone before. On the other hand, a frenzied urge to be different, to change for the sake of change, does not permit the development of a mature style. The current practice of styling for obsolescence depends on novelty for appeal, not on sound design.

However, when a style goes out of fashion, it does not necessarily mean that the design has changed from good to bad. If a design is originally well conceived, it will remain so. It is we who change.

With the changing influences of our time, we often lose the ability to appreciate the art forms of another period or culture, but after a time, they may again have meaning in the current frame of reference. We may not see a work as it was originally seen, but we can find our own pleasure in it. American primitive paintings were for many years unnoticed. Then they were rediscovered by astute collectors. Now there is great demand for these delightfully fresh paintings of people, landscapes, flowers and fruit.

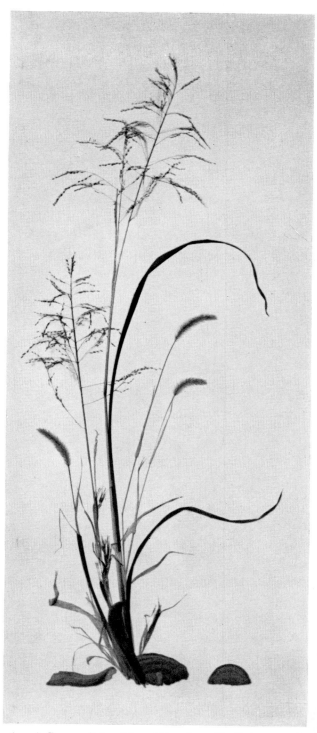

PLATE 6. "Study of Grasses" by Mrs. Theodore E. Guhman. A sensitive, two-dimensional, linear arrangement suggestive of Oriental brush painting. (T. E. Guhman Photo)

Some styles become classic. Generation after generation finds meaning in them. This is true of the traditional styles of Japanese flower arrangement. In the fashion world, compare the timeless beauty of a Worth wedding gown with a high fashion dress of 1929. This would be amusingly out of date if worn today, but the Worth gown would be just as pleasing as it was fifty years ago.

The designer may work in a style ahead of his time, in relation to it or in a conservative traditional way. Whatever the style, to be alive, it must be able to communicate something. *The life of a work of art exists only in the eye of the beholder.*

In *seeing,* that is experiencing, the illustrations in this book, do not be concerned with classifying them as to period or style. It does not matter aesthetically whether a painting is sixteenth-century Italian or an arrangement is Seika. Our purpose here is to experience the formal intent of each artist, and to analyze the design relationships which have been used.

What Is Flower Arranging?

Flower arranging could just as well be called flower *organizing* or flower *composing,* since arranging, organizing and composing all mean the same thing. In this book, I use the words synonymously to mean the *placing of shapes in ordered* relationships. And the word design describes this function in all the arts.

Arranging then is not a distinguishing word, nor is composing nor organizing. The key which sets off flower arranging from the other visual arts must then be the word flower, and not flower in the literal sense but with the broader meaning of flora, that is, all aspects of plant origin and growth. If we keep this larger meaning in mind, we can avoid the frustration of attempting to circumscribe the area of flower arranging.

Actually, the quality which defines an art and distinguishes it from every other art lies not in a term but in the artist's intent and subsequent choice of materials and methods. The intent of flower arranging is to create forms which utilize the *unchanged* materials of nature, with or without related accessories. By unchanged I do not mean that a leaf cannot be clipped or a branch bent to improve the design. I mean

PLATE 7. "Construction No. 2" by Dorothy W. Riester. Handsome pieces of eroded wood were gathered from a lake cove. The variety and sculptured subtlety of their shapes demanded that they be seen, that they be placed together in a design relationship. The bits of wood were organized (composed or arranged), and held together in space by welded steel rods. The new form that emerged from this fitting together of objects found in nature could be classified either as sculpture or as an arrangement. (Ann G. Pass Photo)

that the leaf remains a leaf and the branch a branch. The sculptor may turn wood into a *head* of wood, an architect may make wood into a *house,* but an arranger uses wood very much as it is found in nature.

When a composition no longer contains plant material but is rather a grouping, for example, of pottery or sculpture or craft objects, the composition belongs to another field, display perhaps or interior decoration. On the other hand, when natural materials are used not for their own sake, but to create new shapes, as birds from pine cones or figures from straw, the result belongs in the province of handcraft rather than to flower arranging.

There is a meeting point between the arts. The materials of flower arranging may be used to make wall plaques, collages and other two-dimensional designs, as in Plate 6, or they may be used in three-dimensional sculptural constructions. Plate 7, a construction of natural material, could be termed either sculpture or an arrangement. The art of flower arranging and the art of sculpture have touched at this point. Between these two extremes is a vast field of expression which belongs distinctly to the province of flower arranging.

9

Limitation of Materials

Selection of materials imposes a limitation on form. The connotation of the word limitation, that is, something undesirable or restrictive, does not apply to art. Limitations are one of our greatest aids. Limitations suggest a procedure and stimulate inventiveness. When we work within the full possibilities of what a material will do and what it will not do, the design is benefited.

In Chapter 3, we consider how the shapes, colors and textures of the materials of flower arranging contribute to form. Throughout this book I shall stress, I am sure to the point of tedium, the importance of *experiencing* our materials. Each material offers a unique quality to an arrangement and, while maintaining its individuality, becomes part of a greater new experience. In design, this is just as it is in musical composition, where each sound becomes part of the greater harmony.

A good flower arranger is one who sees, who discovers nature and places her discovery in such a light that others may see it too. To paraphrase Klee's remark, the good arranger will not attempt to reproduce the visible but rather to *make* visible what the unseeing may miss. She will strive in her design to bring out the essential qualities of her materials—the vital, moving growth pattern of a branch; the fragile, satin smoothness of a blossom; the round, exquisite lushness of fruit.

One limitation of the material is due to the mechanics of constructing with it. An artist working in three dimensions has to develop techniques of fastening and supporting. The flower arranger faces the further hazard of dealing with material which is perishable. Containers and holding devices are therefore essential to most arrangements. But you can let these limitations help to direct your design. Work within their possibilities. Accept the structural limitations of your medium just as an architect accepts and creates with the supporting members of footer, beam and joist. An arrangement can also be designed to use the holding members decoratively, or it can conceal them in such a way that their covering is an integrated part of the design. Do not add covering leaves later. This is a major cause of "bottom heaviness" in arrangements. A design should grow, should evolve as a whole, not as a series of makeshifts. Every arranger should have knowledge of mechanical techniques. These influence form, but generally they are matters of fact and not of design. We will therefore not be concerned with them here.

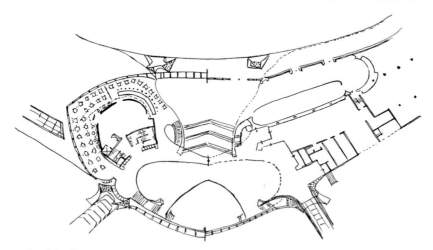

PLATES 8. 9A. 9B. T.W.A. Terminal Model for New York International Airport by Eero Saarinen and Associates, Architects. The flowing expressive form of this building evolved from the relationship of all of its parts; from the floor plan to the space which this creates and divides, to the covering shell. The building developed organically as a flower or fruit, from the seed outward. This is the method of creative design.

ORGANIC GROWTH OF DESIGN

One last definition before we get to the happy business of collecting materials for our arrangements. The term *organic growth,* sometimes expressed as *organic evolution* or *plastic evolution,* is used frequently in creative designing. It refers to the growth principle in nature. Natural growth comes from inner impulse. Its form represents a balance between the forces of inner intent and those of outward modification. The seed of a maple tree has the intent to be a maple tree. The rain, the sun, the soil and man may somewhat modify its form, but the seed will be true to original intent.

This is the principle of life, and the principle which gives life to a design. As with organic growth, each element placed in a design has a function. It is placed where it is and is what it is in relation to another part; this again relates to still another part until a whole form is created.

Examine Figure 1 and Plates 8 to 11. In Eero Saarinen's design for the T.W.A. New York International Airport Terminal, a beautiful evolution of form has been achieved. Each part grows and moves into the larger form in an organic, living way. Notice how the inner space directs the outer form of the building.

The same inner energy can be felt in Seymour Lipton's welded metal sculpture, "Desert Brier" (Plate 10). This is not a reproduction of a plant, but rather an experience in itself. Each part, while maintaining its importance, relates to all the other parts and works with them to make visible the total formal experience.

In the Peruvian weaving (Plate 11), a rich visually exciting pattern has been achieved by alternating and juxtaposing dark and light geometric shapes. The plasticity of the design is so great that we can actually feel our eye moving back and forward, from side to side, in and out. Each shape makes its contribution and moves into the simple unity of the design.

Form created plastically is usually so well integrated that we see it as something spontaneous, even simple, rather than labored and consciously made. This is as it should be. In fact, it is the measure of each art expression. When we see a tree, we see it as the sum total of all its parts. We do not see it as an arrangement of roots, branches, bark and leaves. It is a complete form with a unique character and meaning. Think of the monotony if there were a tree-making formula!

PLATE 10. "Desert Brier" by Seymour Lipton. This sculpture grows from the center outward into the balancing rhythm of its flowerlike form.

Neither formula nor rule can be given for design. A design must grow organically, guided by intent, selectivity and limitation of materials. Basic principles of design can be learned, but they will never give the complete answer. Principles are only the tools of expression, just as words and sentences are the tools of literature. With practice, the use of the tools becomes intuitive. When this occurs, we are on the way to becoming creative designers.

PLATE 11. Peruvian Tapestry Poncho (VIII–X Century). A vivacious design created within a repetitive rectilinear frame. Few geometric shapes have been made into many by placement of contrasting values, shapes and directional movements. The energy of the design comes from within the enclosing frame. (Courtesy, Cooper Union Museum)

Creative designing is a balancing between what we see and feel, and what we can do; between the intuitive and the rational. The great contemporary French artist, Georges Rouault, clearly expresses this inward-outward nature of creating, "In truth, I have painted by opening my eyes day and night on the perceptible world and also by closing them from time to time that I might better see the vision blossom and submit itself to orderly arrangement."

Workshop Lessons

1. Visit an art gallery, museum, and an artist's studio. Request a guided tour or lecture in line with your special interests.
2. For a club program, invite an artist—painter, sculptor, ceramist, architect —to speak to you on his own art.
3. Bring prints of related arts and crafts to class for group discussion. Appoint a leader to direct you in analyzing and comparing the design organizations with those found in natural material of flower arrangements.
4. As a class, analyze the distinguishing differences of trees, plants, and flowers. Let each member deal with a leaf or blossom. Notice the characteristic growth habit, texture, color, shape, scale. Let each one describe what she feels to be the expressive quality of her own material.
5. Discuss the limits of flower arranging (see page 10) both two- and three-dimensional.
6. Experiment with various holding and supporting devices. Use pin holder, wire holder, clay, wax and plastics. Try supporting wire and sticks; devise your own holding methods. Try holding one material by a series of methods. Notice how each method poses limitations and affects the design.

Chapter 2

Materials of Flower Arranging

Human ingenuity can never devise anything more simple and more beautiful or more to the purpose than Nature does. *Leonardo da Vinci*

One small garden plus an imaginative assortment of containers and accessories will provide you with a lifetime of stimulating, varied arrangements. Yet consider how little material you are using in relation to the vast amount available! The materials of flower arranging are as endless as nature itself. Indeed there is such a wealth that we are often at a loss to begin. An unrestricted, limitless field is impossible to design. A selection must be made.

SELECTION OF MATERIAL

Selection may be guided by the requirements of a setting or by your desire to express a mood. Perhaps you have a design problem in mind as, for example, achieving proper balance between fragile blossoms and a heavy stoneware container. Perhaps you are simply proceeding in a kind of "art for art's sake" manner, for the sheer joy of combining shapes, colors and textures. Whatever the approach, you commence a design by choosing materials. This selection must be made with sympathy. This is vital to the total form and expression of the arrangement.

Think Arrangement

Think arrangement in your choosing. A large perfect rose on a straight stem may be beautiful in the garden, but impossible in an arrangement because of its stiffness or size or the relationship of head to stem. For the arranger, it may well remain only an interesting specimen, since she is not concerned with specimen plants but rather with the interest which each flower and leaf and stem will bring to her design.

Consider scale in your choosing. Look for arresting lines in stems and branches; be conscious of the relationship between flower heads, stems and leaves. Imperfections in leaves and flowers often have good design potential. Do not overlook them.

Select materials which are compatible. Relationship by color or texture or variety is often not enough. Materials must belong together in the space and spirit of the arrangement. This may be a belonging by harmony or by contrast. If you have chosen a tall sturdy iris, you will hardly select to go with it a delicate short-stemmed flower like a pansy, even though the flowers relate in color and texture and look well together in the garden. The space and surroundings in a garden are far different from those of an arrangement.

Think arrangement in your seeing, not necessarily a particular arrangement, just arrangement—in the same way that a poet hears words as poetry and a sculptor sees light and shadow in terms of sculpture. If you develop the habit of constant mental selection, you will discover that you have never really seen before. What you once viewed as just a stone or shrub or flower, suddenly assumes a special character. Much of the joy of flower arranging lies in the discovery of the world about us.

Collect Sparingly

Collect flowers sparingly with arrangement in mind. If you pick every flower that interests you, you will find it difficult to decide which to use in your arrangement. You may overcrowd because you "hate to throw anything away." It is always easier to design with too little material than too much. *A limitless field is impossible to design.*

Containers and Accessories

Containers and accessories are part of your design material and must also be chosen with care. Relating them in size, texture, color and shape to your plant material is important but it is not enough. Container and accessory must have an intrinsic quality which belongs in, and contributes to, the total design and experience. Many arrangements are marred by ugly containers. Whether you choose a piece of

PLATE 12.   Ceramic National Exhibition. A varied group of contemporary American ceramics ranging from delicate porcelain bowls to powerful stoneware vases. (Courtesy, Syracuse Museum of Fine Arts—Ann G. Pass Photo)

bent lead, a terra-cotta building block, a slab of wood, a stoneware vase, a metal urn or a porcelain bowl, it must be good in itself.

Accessories may relate in size, color, texture, line and in subject, yet be so inferior, so lacking in taste that it would be better to omit them. Many a Chinese figure, exotic dancer, black panther and cute duck should be left on the shelf.

Good containers and accessories are easy to come by. In recent years there has been a great craft revival. Imaginative pottery, textiles, ceramic sculpture, wood carvings, metal bowls and screens are now shown throughout the country at art fairs, regional exhibitions and craft shops. Execllent museum reproductions of small sculptures and fine ancient bowls are also available. (See Plates 12 to 16.)

PLATE 13. Stoneware Containers by David Weinrib. Imaginative slab-built containers in warm tan stoneware with soft gray-green glaze. (Courtesy, Syracuse Museum of Fine Arts—Ann G. Pass Photo)

Today many arrangers are making their own bowls, vases, stands, figures and backgrounds. This is a natural direction for the creative arranger, a fine extension of her craft. Her work with flowers has

PLATE 14. "Bird Forms" by Dorothy W. Riester. Simple abstracted bird forms of stoneware decorated with earth-colored slips and scriffito. (Ann G. Pass Photo)

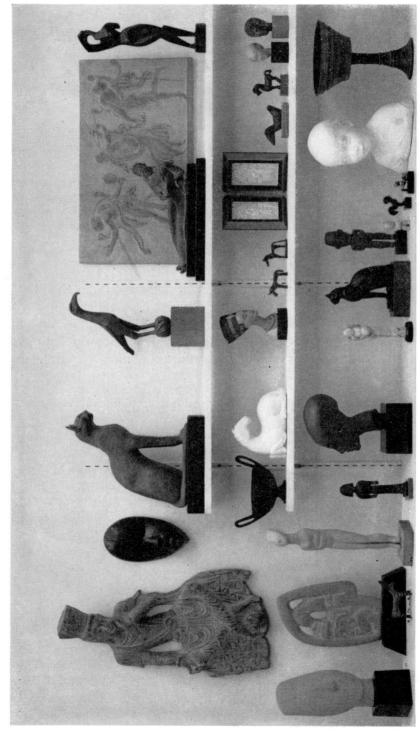

PLATE 15. Museum Reproductions by Alva Studio. A collection of handsomely reproduced art treasures from museums throughout the world.

given her the desire to express herself in related media, and it is hoped that show schedules will encourage this widening of horizons.

In selecting container or accessory, be aware of the emphasis you wish to place on it in your design. You may want to minimize it so that it goes almost unnoticed in your arrangement. In this case, do not look for contrasts but for harmonizing relationships. The round dish in Plate 19 and the stone base in Plate 29 are integrated parts of the designs, yet they are subordinate. On the other hand, an unusual

PLATE 16. "Yucca Pods in Pre-Columbian Bowl" by Esther Wheeler. An ancient Mexican shape has directed the character of this arrangement. (Boutrelle-Sevecke Photo)

container or perhaps a piece of sculpture can be so stimulating that it directs the choice of all other materials and remains dominant in the design, as the basket in Plate 20, the sculpture in Plate 17, the straw figure in Plate 18, or the pre-Columbian bowl in Plate 16.

Your containers and accessories may be purchased or improvised, found or made. Whatever the source, choose them with care. A design will not be better than any of its parts.

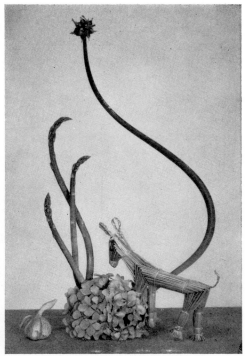

PLATE 17. "Figure with Amaryllis" by Mrs. Norman Able and Mrs. James W. Kinnear, Jr. The strong, simple, terra-cotta figure, made by Mrs. Kinnear's daughter, has inspired the selection of material and the design of the arrangement. (Boutrelle-Sevecke Photo)

PLATE 18. "Donkey" by Mrs. William E. Seibel. The straw figure was made by the arranger and was the inspiration for this whimsical composition. (William E. Seibel Photo)

NATURAL ELEMENTS

Now let us consider natural materials. Let us discover the unique quality which they bring to our arrangements, how they set the design process into motion, and what they teach us about ourselves. Let us put aside for a time the problems of designing any one arrangement and go into a garden, field or woodland to observe nature. We should go in the spirit of adventure, as seekers and collectors with eyes and mind open to the world about us.

First of all, feel and observe. Feel the changing moods of light and shifting shadows on the lawn or forest floor. Observe the restless

PLATE 19. "Woodland Pool" by Mrs. Harold D. Warren. The illusion in this composition is so complete that the white plate is not a base or a container but actually a pool. (Panda Photography)

PLATE 20. "Baskets with Chrysanthemums" by Margaret Carrick. The strong dark base and the two light chrysanthemums emphasize the delicate curving baskets. (Jack Carrick Photo)

24

movement of growth, the shapes, colors, textures and design relationships. A leaf unfolding, a bud opening is a beautiful evolution of form.
The balance-counterbalance placement of the branches of a tree is a
study in rhythm, and the relationship of blossom to stem and stem to
ground is a perfectly achieved transition.

Observe, too, the repetition of design patterns which occur through
nature. The radiating crystals of Plate 24, the coral in Plate 23 and
the spoon chrysanthemum in Plate 20 have a marked similarity of pattern, even though they are unrelated in other ways. The same radiat-

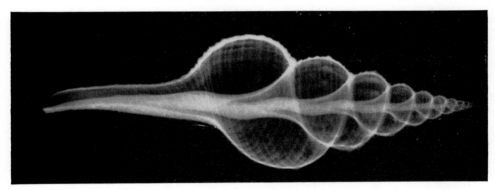

PLATE 21. X-ray of a Shell. The X-ray reveals the inner necessity which determined the outer shape of the shell. The inner design demonstrates the rhythms and
order of organic growth. (Courtesy, Eastman Kodak Company)

ing design may be observed on the underside of a mushroom, in the
web of a spider or the veining of a leaf. The discovery of design relationships is valuable training in seeing and a source of imaginative
combinations for future arrangements.

Nature on Your *Terms*

Going to nature does not necessarily mean that we will find there a
readymade assortment of compositions. Nor does it mean that we will
carry out the solution found in nature. We are creating in a different
space, under different limitations and for a different purpose. Often
a flower which normally grows close to the ground may be better placed
high in our composition except, of course, in classic Japanese work.
Or we may have a collection of materials which could not possibly grow
together but are compatible in the created environment of the arrangement, for example, the forced horse chestnut and amaryllis in Plate 17.

PLATE 22.   X-ray of a Rose. Here is shown the great beauty of the opening flower, its subtle transition into the line of the stem and the rhythmic balance of stems, leaves and veins. (Courtesy, Eastman Kodak Company)

PLATE 23. X-ray of Coral. The radiating pattern of the coral is common in nature and in design usage. Notice in this seemingly simple shape the variety in spacing and emphasis. The longer you study it, the more variations you will find. (Courtesy, Eastman Kodak Company)

PLATE 24. Radiating Group of Natrolite Crystals. Compare this radiating design in nature with the pattern of both the basket and the chrysanthemums in Plate 20. (Courtesy, American Museum of Natural History)

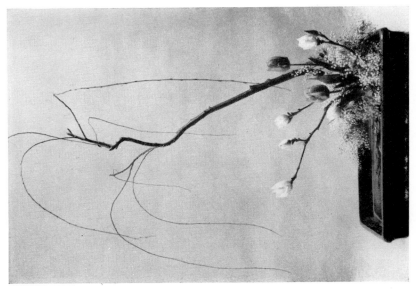
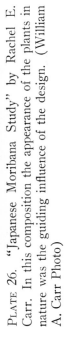

PLATE 26. "Japanese Moribana Study" by Rachel E. Carr. In this composition the appearance of the plants in nature was the guiding influence of the design. (William A. Carr Photo)

PLATE 25. "Flemish Arrangement" by Mrs. William F. Lowry, Jr. Here the primary interest lies in the rich color of the material and the variety of shapes and textures. (Bouttrelle-Sevecke Photo)

Recall the opening quotation from Santayana, "Nature must reply to me in my own terms." You can respect plant growth and learn from it, as you see relationships in nature. Let these stimulate your imagination, but do not hesitate to bend or prune or regroup to further the organization and expression of your design.

Contribution of Material

Compare Plates 25 and 26. One is inspired by the Flemish Baroque way of seeing and using the materials of nature as a flamboyancy of textures and colors. The Moribana arrangement illustrates the Japanese use of materials to create a feeling of serenity and give the look of natural growth. In each case, the arranger has felt and observed, has freely cut and bent and grouped to create the ordered space and the expression which was desired.

We should be aware of the special characteristics of materials and allow each to give its own message. Notice the richness and intricacy of the texture and shape of the container, the flowers and leaves in Plate 25. Each has an expressive power which contributes to the whole experience of the design. In Plate 26, the shining water, dark cool pebbles, soft mimosa, tulips, magnolia and graceful willow branch evoke an appropriate response. If maple branches and white chrysanthemums had been used in the same design relationship as the willow and tulips, the expression would be different. *Each material has a unique contribution to make.*

Sometimes one material is of such interest that it is given the dominant role in the design as the smoothly polished, cool, striated marble of Brancusi's "Fish" in Plate 27. Perhaps you may see a flower or a branch so distinctive that you will wish to use it alone. Then arrangement will be the balanced relationship between this one flower or branch, the container, and the space around it, as in Plates 20 and 28.

Inspiration from Material

Choose materials which spark your imagination and are expressive of *you.* If you do not respond to the flowers which you arrange, how can you expect anyone else to? Do not be afraid to use any material which interests you. There is no such thing as a good or bad shape in nature, or one that is appropriate or inappropriate. We are the ones that make it so by what we do with it, and beauty is often unexpected.

Mariska Karasz, the well-known embroidery designer, has described with excitement the discovery of a piece of binding twine which had come on a package. This she embroidered into one of her handsome hangings. The common fuzzy twine became beautiful in its appropriateness and expressive contribution to the design. When some-

PLATE 27. "Fish" by Constantin Brancusi. One magnificently simple shape in striated, polished marble has been placed in space in such a way that we fully experience its nature and beauty. (Courtesy, Museum of Modern Art)

thing becomes marvelous and complete, it is beautiful. Arrangers are discovering beauty not only in familiar materials but in stones and wood and seeds, in a host of unexpected places. *Beauty is where you find it.*

Larger Relationships

It is impossible to see one object by itself. We see everything in relation to the space and to the other objects around it. As you collect material, it is wise to observe the larger setting and the objects closely surrounding the material which you chose. A leaf which appears small with a smooth, blue-green sheen in the garden may only be dwarfed there by larger, coarse leaves and appear blue by reflecting the sky. In

PLATE 28. "Apple Blossoms" by Mrs. Joseph E. Wolff. A hanging antique jug holding a curve of flowering branch makes a complete statement for us to experience and enjoy. (J. E. Wolff Photo)

the new environment of the arrangement, the same leaf may appear large, rough, and of yellow-green hue.

It often happens that it is the relationship that appeals to us, not the object. Autumn leaves are never as breath-takingly beautiful in an arrangement as they are when seen against a brilliant sky or edged by a dark thicket of evergreens. To avoid being disappointed in your dis-

PLATE 29. "Study in Green" by Mrs. Howard Oberlin. Unlikely material for an arrangement—skunk cabbage and onion heads—has been freshly seen and its beauty communicated. (Howard Oberlin Photo)

PLATE 30. "St. Francis" by Mrs. Thomas Mairs. Each material speaks for itself and the total expression is one of reverence for nature. (Bryan Studio)

coveries when you bring them home, take time to feel and observe them in their larger environment.

When we observe natural relationships, we are storing up ideas for the future. For example, we may notice how grasses bend in the wind and how the lowest blades curl and relate to the ground. This memory may guide the movement and relationships of a future arrangement.

PLATE 31. "Aspen Trees." Nature is full of these accidental rhythms of lines and textures which we can see if we are looking for them. (Walter Manderfield Photo)

The soft green mosses and crisp rows of lichens around an ancient log may suggest another composition, or perhaps it will be the riotous blending of colors in a summer garden which inspires us to experiment with new and exciting color relationships.

The observation of a row of trees like the aspens in Plate 31 can be a storehouse of ideas, any one of which may consciously or subconsciously be used later. We may be impressed by the crossing and weaving of diagonal branches through heavier vertical trunks, and notice how this diagonal movement is balanced by the light which moves behind the trees and in the opposite direction. We may remember the small textural clump of leaves on the left. We see that the trees do not spring from one point but from a horizontal line and in an interesting

PLATE 32. "Bad Lands." Erosion patterns in land and wood and rocks are nature's sculpture, surpassing our most vivid imaginings. (Alicia Parry Photo)

variety of groupings. We notice, too, the space divisions which are as exciting as the trees themselves. The movement of light to dark and back to light is a dramatic spatial use of light that can be applied directly to an arrangement. Also we may be inspired by colors and sounds, fragrances and movement of the wind, which we would experience if we were actually on this wooded mountain side.

This is true also of the arid "Bad Lands" in Plate 32. There is much to observe in the photograph which will be of value in our design experience. We notice the light, and how it intensifies the volumetric shapes of the land, how it helps to relate the shapes and carry our eye forward and back and around through space. The textures are especially interesting and also the repetitive pattern of the eroded pyramidal shapes which move together in an endless variety of ways. In some places, they form a repetitive border, in others they overlap. They vary in size and grouping, but all relate to the total landscape. What a compositional lesson this is to the arranger who is working with one material.

Much of what we observe will not consciously affect a specific arrangement but will become part of our appreciation and the fund of knowledge which guides our creative work. The art of observation requires practice and use, and it is most difficult to see beyond the details to the large simplified relationships. By developing the capacity to see each element as part of a larger relationship, we are developing a talent essential to successful designing—the ability to see the whole.

Lessons from Collecting

In this survey of the nature of our materials, I have suggested that selection be restricted only by a general sense of arrangement, and by the interest which materials instill in us. So we learn while collecting and the findings from a field trip tell us a great deal about ourselves. It may reveal that we are timid, afraid to accept a challenge, that we lack imagination or perhaps have a poor color sense. Are your selections always based on something that you have seen others use, or have you had the adventure of discovering something of your own? I do not suggest that you will discover new, never-seen-before species, but rather that you will see something that has always been there, but in a way that makes seeing a personal experience.

An artist once described to me her unforgettable experience of *discovering* Notre Dame. She had not rushed to it on her first day in Paris as a sight to see, but rather had allowed the city to reveal itself gradually to her. Notre Dame was discovered quite by chance on an afternoon's walk. It was a magnificent experience. She had not looked *at* the cathedral as a sight but rather had *experienced* it in a way that made it truly her own.

PLATE 33. "Cecropia" by Mrs. Robert Eickelburger. The variations of a single type of leaf offer more than enough interest for one design. (Ken Eargle Photo)

It takes time to see. Allow time for the true nature of your material to reveal itself to you.

If twenty people are collecting, there will then be twenty distinctly different collections. Even when the collecting is limited to one locale, there will be individual preferences. One person may be interested in leaves and select those that relate to stem or branch in an interesting way; another may choose them for unusual shape, texture or even imperfections. The selection may include a number of varieties, or a single species may offer more than enough variations of compelling interest, as the cecropia leaves in Plate 33.

One collector may be inspired by color, another by the time of day or season of the year or by indigenous plants. We are individuals with different tastes, reactions and interests, and these are subject to change as we grow, gain new insight and meet new needs. Although we all organize our materials by the same basic methods, the final expression differs just as we differ. Design is a highly personal affair. Analyze your collections; they will tell you a great deal about yourself, your preference, your lacks, your enthusiasms. We must meet and trust ourselves before we can design creatively because design comes from within.

Workshop with Materials

Plan collecting trips to specified places—a particular garden, woods, a field, a road side, a produce yard. Bring your collection from a given locale to class for critical evaluation and working problems. (If the work room is small, don't bring too much.) Here are some problems which have proved stimulating:

1. Display materials separately so that others can see the interest which you saw. Compare their reactions to yours.
2. Experiment with combinations of materials. Loosely hold in your hand, or place on the table combinations and varying amounts of your materials in order to experience how shapes, colors and textures go together. (Do this in the way decorators assemble shapes and swatches of material to determine the relationships which will later be used in a room.) Since you are not formally arranging, freely try every possible combination, even ones which you think may be bad. These are often the ones which spark the imagination and lead to departures in your arranging.
3. Exchange materials. Try combining yours with those of other class members.

4. When you find something interesting, as a particular grouping or color combination or spacing, stop and discuss it. Experience and analyze the materials separately and in groupings.
5. Develop several arrangements from ideas which the materials have suggested.
6. Create an arrangement inspired by the associations of the place where the collection was made.
7. Bring to class for study and critical analysis a variety of imaginative, well-chosen containers and accessories. Analyze the aesthetic and design quality of each.

N.B. In your studying and experimenting, *be relaxed;* do not approach arranging with fixed ideas or a do-or-die attitude. Allow it to reveal itself to you; enjoy the work and discipline of creating.

Chapter 3

Design Analysis of Materials

Simplicity is not an end in art, but one arrives at simplicity in spite
of oneself in approaching the real sense of things.   *Constantin Brancusi*

The language of design is universal and timeless because its symbols and principles remain constant. Design is based on optics, on how
we see, how we nervously react to all that crosses our field of vision,
on our ability to abstract the countless forms about us into simple geometric shapes. These reactions and abilities have altered little over the
centuries.

A child is born with a mechanism for seeing and perceiving, but he
must learn to use these abilities, and the learning is a life-long, growing
process. When an individual learns to see only well enough to satisfy
his physical requirements, the understanding and the making of art
are impossible for him. Design is a language which we learn to understand by training our eyes to see and our consciousness to perceive.
We can design only when we learn to see—it is one and the same.

Visual Symbols

Every shape in nature can be abstracted into a geometric symbol.
Thus one flower may be seen as a sphere, another as a square, a third
as a triangle. Geometric shapes speak to us all in the same general
way; they have a common communicative meaning. Therefore, they
become visual symbols. A designer learns to see the abstract symbolic
elements in all materials, and then uses them as basic units of design.

Plates 34, 35, and 36 show three art forms from widely separated
periods in history, yet in each we easily discern basic similarity in
shape. We easily follow the rhythms of the design relationships. We
can see in each art form how the subject matter has been abstracted
into a larger rhythmic pattern. The stylized human figure and lions

forming the Persian pole top in Plate 34 remarkably resemble the formalized urns of flowers in the French eighteenth-century wallpaper of Plate 35. The repetitive pattern of the stylized, texturally-rich leaves forming the Romanesque capital in Plate 36 is organized

PLATE 34. Persian Pole Top (VI–IV Century B.C.). The stylized human figure bears a design resemblance to all compositions which are organized in this same general way. The ancient figure is very like contemporary work in its abstraction and emphasis on space. (Courtesy, Metropolitan Museum of Art)

in the same allover pattern as the French paper. The individual leaves resemble both the Persian bronze and the wallpaper detail. Further examination will reveal other similarities in shape and design relationships.

UNITS OF DESIGN

Various hypotheses have been advanced as to what constitutes a basic geometric unit. In ancient India the basic unit was the magic square. Aristotle believed that all shapes were derived from a square and a sphere. More recently, the French painter, Paul Cézanne, considered the cone, the cylinder and the sphere as basic, while Wassily Kandinsky, also an early twentieth-century painter, chose the smallest visual unit—a point. From this he showed how line and plane and eventually all shapes evolved.

Most contemporary designers think of their basic working units in terms of point, line, plane, texture, color and a sixth tangible-intangible element, space. These elements combine to form the shape of all matter. Each makes a unique contribution. Yet it cannot be

PLATE 35. French Wallpaper (XVIII Century). In this design, natural shapes have been stylized and freely used for the larger purpose of the composition. Notice the interesting way in which scale is changed. In one repeat, flowers are larger than the carillon; in the other, they are in scale with the container. An artist is free to create his own world of imagination. (Courtesy, Cooper Union Museum)

PLATE 36. Romanesque Capital (French XII Century). A repetitive use of stylized leaves. The individual leaves are enriched with decorative veining, flowers and plants. (Courtesy, Metropolitan Museum of Art)

divorced from space nor seen for long as a separate unit. However, for the purpose of study, we will examine each element alone.

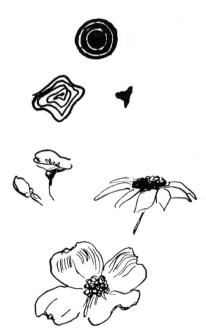

FIG. 1. Point, any inward moving shape

THE POINT

A point is the *smallest* and the *strongest* visual symbol in design. It *commands* attention because its directional movement is inward to a central focal spot. A point does not have to be perfectly round, it can be any free or geometric shape so long as the direction is inward and static as in Figure 1. The majority of flowers are seen as points. The amaryllis in Plate 17 and the violets and Solomon's-seal in Plate 19 are points.

The pull of a point is so great that an arranger may use a single pointlike flower or leaf to balance a much larger shape as the onion head in Plate 18. Notice the moon in Henri Rousseau's painting, "Carnival Evening" (Plate

PLATE 37. "Carnival Evening" by Henri Rousseau. The pull of the moon on two lone figures, the quiet horizontal line of earth and clouds and the restless lines of the trees have made this a night of mystery. (Courtesy, Louis E. Stern)

37). A point can be so strong that it will stop all movement except for the inward pull which it attracts to itself.

So that the two equal points will not compete for attention, cover half the moth in Plate 38, and you will experience the compelling static pull of the point wing marking.

PLATE 38. "Moth." A symmetrical design in nature of irregularly shaped and accented round point markings. (Dr. Edward Degginger Photo)

Focal Point and "to Point"

A point as a basic unit should not be confused with the term *focal point,* as this is commonly understood by arrangers. Their focal point is generally a massing of shapes, which may or may not be points, into one dominant area in the design. The area is usually not a point because it is of a size to give directional movement *other than inward.* Compare the lively use of points in Odilon Redon's "Vase of Flowers" (Plate 39) and the static focal point, or focal area, in Figure 2.

We should not confuse *to point* with *a* point. To point implies a directional line of movement, a pointing arrow as opposed to the static dotlike shape of a point.

PLATE 39. "Vase of Flowers" by Odilon Redon. All the flowers and leaves in the painting are pointlike in shape. Their placement, varying sizes and values create a lively design. (Courtesy, Cleveland Museum of Art —Bequest of Leonard C. Hanna, Jr.)

FIG. 2. Focal-point cliché

PLATE 40. "Nebulosity in Monoceros." The stars, even under the most power-ful telescope, are small points in the heavens. (Courtesy, American Museum of Natural History—Mt. Wilson Photo)

Relevancy of Point

The majority of flowers are pointlike in shape but how we see them depends on the distance at which we view them. Far away a large shape, as a ship on the horizon, appears to be a point. We see stars as pinpoints in the sky. Even when greatly magnified, as in the cone nebula of Plate 40, we still see stars as points because of their great distance. The leaves of a tree usually appear as points until closely observed. Then they usually become planes with a definite direction, as in Figure 3a.

Conversely, it happens that we can only see some points when we are close to them. In Plate 41 the beach is a plane edged by the sea until we look closely and discover that it is made up of myriads of points of sand, and so with flowers. In the garden, we may see them as part of the linear movement of their stems, but in the closeness of an arrangement, each flower head may become a forceful point as in Plate 39 or Plate 42.

PLATE 41. "Sand and Rocks." The grains of sand are so small and so many that we would have to examine them under a microscope to see their individual pointlike nature. (Walter Manderfield Photo)

A flower may be pointlike at a distance but when viewed closer, only the center or true flower may retain the quality of a point, as in Figure 3b. In Plate 42 the outer petals may move into an entirely different relationship. In one arrangement, they may relate to other groupings in color, texture and directional movement, but the center of the flower would remain a point drawing the eye inward. In another arrangement the cactus could be placed with larger shapes and in such a relationship that the entire flower might function as a point in the design. A designer should always remember that *all is relative to the specific conditions created in each design.*

Points are powerful tools in design. They bring stability, variety and tensional excitement as they arrest our vision from the quick movements of the composition and hold us in momentary suspension. Learn to recognize point in all your material. It may be in the form of the apple blossoms, in the leaves and chain links as in Plate 28 or the leaves and berries in Plate 43. Point can be a decoration on a container or fabric. Recognize points so that you can control them and make them work for you in the total experience of arrangement.

(a) (b)

FIG. 3. Point relative to size and distance. a. Most leaves are pointlike at a distance. b. Flowers as a whole, or only the centers, can be seen as points.

PLATE 42. "Desert Cactus." A perfect design radiating from a central pivotal point to a rough-textured point, composed of a series of points, to the final circle of overlapping filmy petals. Variations of the design in nature can be found in many compositions. (Dr. Edward Degginger Photo)

LINE

Line is motion. Motion is an intrinsic quality of all the symbols of expression, whether it be the movement of the body in dance, the tongue and the lips in speaking, or the eyes in reading. A point, even while it holds our eye, is creating a path of motion from our eye to its

PLATE 43. "Columns and Ivy" by Mrs. Raymond R. Stoltz. The line of ivy which we see is not the line of its stem but the irregular line of the leaves. (Boutrelle-Sevecke Photo)

center. When a second point is placed in relation to the first point, a new directional movement is created as our eye is pulled back and forth between the two points. The motion is the line. The line can be made visible and forced to move in any direction by adding more points as in Figure 4. As the points move closer together, they lose their individual pull and the eye runs smoothly along in their directional path.

In an arrangement, line is frequently created in just such a way. This can be clearly seen in the ivy leaves and snow berries in Plate 43.

Variations in Line

Variations in line as found in nature or created by the designer are endless. A line may move quickly or slowly. Consider the change of tempo in the main directional line in the arrangement in Plate 44. The movement is at first quite slow through the heavy base point shapes, then faster over the closely bunched points of the berries, then to a final quick climax of the smoothly-continuous upper lines.

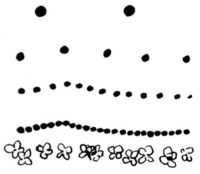

FIG. 4. Line, evolution from point

Piet Mondrian's "Horizontal Tree" (Plate 45) is a spatial balance between quickly moving continuous lines and broken, stable, horizontal and vertical lines. "Improvisation, Number 23" by Kandinsky, Plate 46, has tremendous variety and vitality of line. The lines are thick, thin, broken, straight, curved, crossing, fast, slow, visible and invisible. The invisible lines are the paths between the tensional points in the painting. Notice in Plate 47 how the eye makes many unrecorded invisible paths between the flowers, the twigs, the branch tips and the pointlike opening in the base. With this there is a great variety of recorded lines—the irregular line of the base, the smooth subtle line of the vase, the blurred variegated line of the flowers and the constantly changing rich statement of the branch lines. Plate 48 illustrates how a series of lines moving in one direction can be placed in a repetitive relationship to create another line perpendicular to the shorter individual lines. The trees in Plate 37 and the "Goslings" individually move vertically but in a series they create a horizontal line.

Expressiveness of Line

The rhythmic, living quality of line makes it, with color, one of the most expressive elements in design. The arranger may suggest many moods through the direction and various tempos of line. Look again at Plates 43 through 48 which illustrate types of line. The emotional expression which each work conveys is different. There are, of course, other elements entering into this total expression, but the dominant influence is line.

PLATE 44. Arrangement for Alcoa Office by Mrs. William F. Lowry, Jr. A design of many kinds of lines ranging from the slow choppy lines composed from the point fruit and berries, to the quick explosive line of the rushes and the gay curving line of the pods and container. (Associated Photographers)

Compare the mystery and quiet serenity of "Carnival Evening" with the vital active branches in "Horizontal Tree" and the stately almost mechanical motion of "Goslings." Each artist has used a predominantly horizontal composition; the expression is different because the kinds of line and their spatial relationships are different. I point this out because the statement has frequently been made that horizontal lines express repose. They may, and often do, *if this is the designer's intent.*

PLATE 45. "Horizontal Tree" by Piet Mondrian. Dancing, moving rhythms of growth against the stable horizontal line of the earth and the vertical human axis of orientation. (Courtesy, Munson-Williams-Proctor Institute)

PLATE 46. "Improvisation No. 23" by Wassily Kandinsky. This painting creates an emotional experience through the use of quickly moving lines, color and point tensions which are akin to our feelings while listening to music. (Courtesy, Munson-Williams-Proctor Institute)

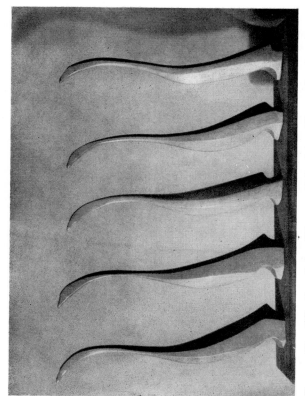

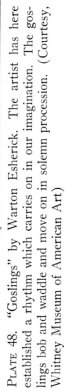

PLATE 48. "Goslings" by Warton Esherick. The artist has here established a rhythm which carries on in our imagination. The goslings bob and waddle and move on in solemn procession. (Courtesy, Whitney Museum of American Art)

PLATE 47. "Nageire Arrangement" by Rachel E. Carr. "One arrives at simplicity in spite of oneself in approaching the real sense of things." Brancusi. (William A. Carr Photo)

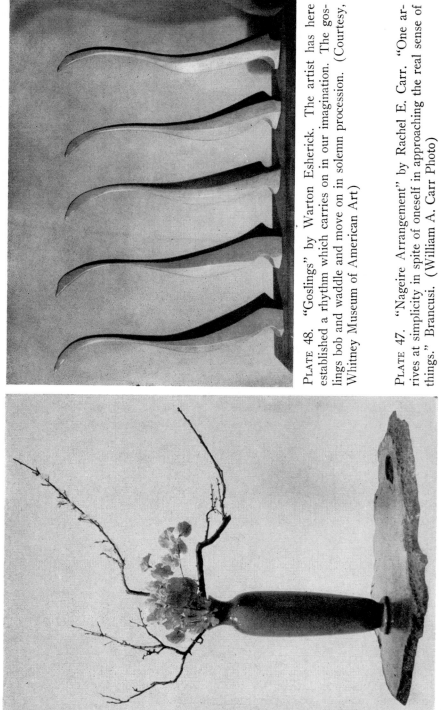

54

PLATE 49. "Study of Lilies" by Mrs. Fred J. Hay. The narrow linear shape of the leaves, petals and vase decoration have been combined in a seemingly effortless design. The sense of ease attests to the success of the design. (Carolina Studios)

We have also noticed that vertical lines frequently give a feeling of aspiration. This again is relative. Plate 43 is a vertical arrangement yet the feeling is more of the earth, of the horizontal plane, because of the emphasis of the bird and the lower cluster of white berries. Cover these and the line emphasis—and consequently the expressiveness—changes. The autumn arrangement in Plate 44 (particularly when the sobering shapes at the lower right are covered) has the explosively gay, dancing rhythms that curved and diagonal lines can give. The central portion of both Kandinsky's painting (Plate 46) and this arrangement have much in common. Both make use of the expressive power of line. The quiet horizontal and vertical dignity in the Nageire arrangement, Plate 47, with its contrasting soft flowers and restless lines, creates much the same mood—and by the same methods—as "Carnival Evening" (Plate 37). The dark point at the base of the arrangement can almost be seen as a reversal of the white moon in the painting.

Generally, we can say that horizontal lines give serenity, that vertical lines inspire, that crossed vertical and horizontal lines create stability. Notice how Mondrian has used this type of line in Plate 45. Curved and spiraling lines can be graceful, while diagonal and jagged lines are exciting, disturbing, restless. Notice in Plate 37 the sense of foreboding that Rousseau has introduced at the right of the figures with the diagonal and crossing tree branches. There is this feeling also in the paintings of El Greco. Plate 46 is charged with restless excitement. This same feeling is found in many of the early Japanese arrangements.

These are but an obvious few of the many emotional subtleties which can be expressed by the language of line.

Types of Line

We have been speaking of line in the broad sense of being a path of directional movement. The movement may be implied, continuous or broken, as in Figure 5a, b and c. When we study the arrangement in Plate 49, we travel at various tempos over many kinds of lines. In Figure 5a, pointlike shapes draw us along invisible lines; in Figure 5b, we follow the quick solid line of stem and container; in Figure 5c, it is easy to follow the broken line created by leaves and petals.

Lines of Composition and Continuance

So far we have considered lines as separate experiences, unrelated to each other and to their ultimate role as unifying members of the design. In this capacity, a line is often referred to as of a specific kind, as *line of composition*. In this sense, line refers to the main movement. It may be created from the movement of a branch or a stem, as in Plate 49, or it may be a visual path created by the grouping of many smaller shapes as in Plate 44. In Figure 5d, the line of the arrangement becomes a gentle reverse curve moving from base of vase to tip of stem. It becomes the axial pivot supporting the movement-countermovement of the design. Many of these movements are seen as *lines of continuance*, as in Figure 5e.

A line of continuance is a movement that is implemented not by one more or less constant line, but by a series of stimuli and directional pulls and pushes. It is often largely unrecorded. When a directional signal is given, the eye will leap across shapes with differing directional movements and through large areas of space. The focal pulls, which direct the line of continuance, are predominantly color, point and the momentum of an established movement.

Notice in Plate 49 how the eye follows the established direction of the line, up the left side of the vase, along the under edge of the lily, along a leaf edge to the lily on the far right. Other petals and leaves with counter movements cross the line, but they do not interfere with

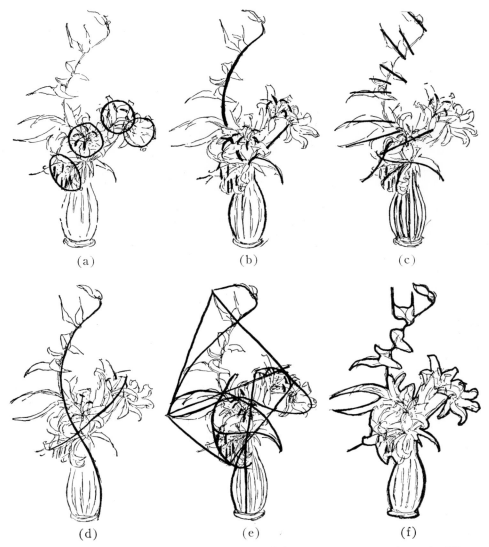

(a) (b) (c)

(d) (e) (f)

Fig. 5. Types of lines. a. Line as an invisible path between points. b. Direct recorded line. c. Line from directional movement of repetitive shapes. d. Line as main directional movement of a composition. e. Lines of continuance. f. Line as outer boundary of a shape—"outline."

this established path. When the line reaches the lily on the right, a choice must be made. The eye can leap from the farthest petal across the intervening space in the directional line of the tip bud, or it may follow the circular broken lines of the stamens around the curved outline of the lilies, and so on to its origin.

In the leisurely enjoyment of the arrangement, the eye will follow both lines of continuance plus many others. If the arrangement is turned, a new network of lines will present themselves as new relationships are established. This is why an arranger must seek the continuing lines on all sides of her design.

PLATE 50. "Frieze of Dancers" by Hilaire-Germain Edgar Degas. Every work of art is created many times. Degas first created this painting when he placed on his canvas the rhythms of line, color and plane. We recreate the experience each time we see and relive the orders of the painting. (Courtesy, Cleveland Museum of Art—Gift of Hanna Fund)

Allow your eye to follow the paths created by the movement of the skirts, heads, arms, feet, hands and shadows in Degas' "Frieze of Dancers" (Plate 50). You will find a web of lines weaving up and down, backward and forward, in and out of space. This web both creates and binds the elements of the painting. We shall see later the value of lines of continuance in design organization.

Outlines

An *outline* is the outer edge, the boundary of shapes. The shape which the outline defines may be the shape of the whole arrangement, as in Figure 5f, or it may be the shape of some object in the arrangement, as a leaf, a flower, a container. Or the outline may be the boundary of spatial shapes like those created by the lines of continuance in Figure 5e. In this case, the lines of continuance also act as outlines. The shapes which we see enclosed by outline, whether tangible shapes of objects or intangible shapes of space, are seen as planes.

PLANE

Everything we refer to as a shape is technically a plane or combination of planes. *A plane is any two dimensional area enclosed by line.* Following the theory that all shapes evolve from point, let us place three pebbles in a triangular relationship, as in Figure 6a. The eye automatically draws a line between the pebbles, as in Figure 6b, thereby enclosing an area which is then a plane, Figure 6c.

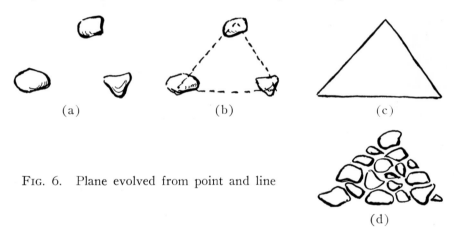

(a)   (b)   (c)

FIG. 6.   Plane evolved from point and line

(d)

We may also create a plane by massing together a number of points, as in Figure 5d or in Plate 51. In any case, the plane is enclosed by an *outline* which moves between terminal points.

Flower arrangers compose with the planes of their selected materials; they also create planes in compositions by this basic method. In Plate 52, there is a series of planes moving from the horizontal of the table top to the base, and then on by a series of triangular planes to the tip leaf. Figure 7 diagrams the major planes in this arrangement. You will notice that one spatial plane is made by the three pivotal flowers, that the large plane at the base is made up of not one leaf, but a grouping of leaves, of flowers and glass culets. All of these form an area with the same directional movement.

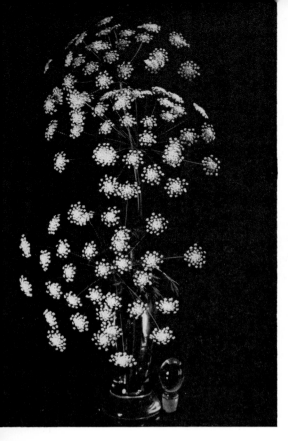

PLATE 51. "Queen Anne's Lace" by Mrs. J. R. M. Wilson. A starry, jewel-like design of many small points of flowers has been created in nature. The arranger has grouped three of these radiating flower clusters to make one form of even greater interest and beauty. (Panda Photography)

Planes can be of any shape. They do not have to be flat as a table or wall. They may have variations of surface and may bend slightly. However, when the distortion reaches the point where a third dimension is indicated, the original plane must break into two or more planes with different directional movements because *a plane is always a two-dimensional area.*

In Plate 52, notice the place (above the third flower) where the curving leaves change plane direction. The line which marks the break in the plane becomes the main directional line of the arrangement. *The edges of planes are lines,* and they are valuable in creating and carrying along the main directional movements in design.

Depth through Plane

The directional movement of planes is one of the most important ways of creating, of making visible, the third dimension, or the sense of depth in a design. Front, side, top, bottom, inside, even the idea of back, are made visible by the movement of planes in space. The eye readily detects the spatial movement of planes by means of converging lines and by light and shadow. As a plane moves away from the field of vision, less and less of its surface is seen, and the side lines, which originally had a perpendicular relationship to the bottom line, move together or converge towards an imaginary point in space. Notice how the shape of the blossoms in the central clump of Queen Anne's lace (Plate 51) changes from round, to oval, to line, as the flower heads tip away from our field of vision. If it were not for this convergence, we would be unable to see the round, three-dimensional shape of the flowers.

Generally, a directional shift in plane is accompanied by a change in light value. This is pronounced when light comes from one source, as in the lily arrangement (Plate 49). We can easily see the three-dimensional shape of the vase, the lilies, and of the whole arrangement because of the movement of the planes into and away from the light. Observe in the Degas painting (Plate 50) the way in which the figures, and the space which they occupy, are realized in planes of dark and light. There is a plastic, tactile movement of planes in and out of space. This gives a dimension of depth to this painting.

Three-dimensional shapes are made up of a series of planes—front, side, back, top, bottom. In all three-dimensional designing, it is important to see the movement of the planes *around* an object. The outline shows the arrangement as a two-dimensional plane, as in Figure 5f. To find depth, we must look within the frame for the many changing directions of planes in space. The subtle three-dimensional shape of Brancusi's "Fish" (Plate 27) and of the vase in Plate 47 is seen mainly because of the converging of the inner planes away from the light into shadow.

Volume and Volumetric Shapes

When three-dimensional shapes are not solid, like an apple or a stone, but are open, as a room or a container, they are called volumetric shapes, and the space enclosed by the walls of the planes is referred to as volume. There is a difference in the feeling of weight between solid and volumetric shapes. Compare the volumetric lilies in Plate 49 and the solid fruit in Plate 44. Each makes a different contribution and demands a different use in design. Learn to recognize the volumetric shapes in nature, as curled leaves and bell-shaped, cupped and trumpeted flowers.

PLATE 52. "Spiral of Leaves and Flower" by Mrs. Howard S. Kittel. Our eye is moved steadily upward from the horizontal base to the final vertical leaf by a series of overlapping, bending and turning planes. (Lawrence Joseph Photo)

Texture

Now let us look at the elements of texture and color. These have to do with the *surface* of objects. They are often so appealing in themselves that the eye is tricked into seeing only the surface and not the underlying form. This camouflage is put to good use in nature. I am always startled when a lumpy brown toad suddenly leaps from a spot of earth and leaves, or a yellow warbler glides from an autumn branch.

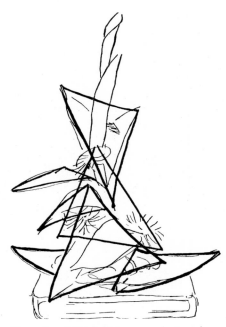

FIG. 7. Overlapping and turning planes create volume and depth

Texture is the covering skin, it is the *touch quality* of an object. The designer of articles to be handled, fabrics or utensils, is always conscious of the actual *feel* of his material. An arranger uses texture only as a visual element. Indeed, there are a number of textures repellent to the touch but interesting to look at, as those of a thistle, a rose stem, or a bur.

Children learn a great deal about the world through the sense of touch. They experience softness, smoothness, hardness, sharpness, stickiness by touching. Their elementary sensations are later transferred through knowledge and imagination into *visual touching.* We

PLATE 54. "Teasel Weed." Sharp jagged thorns, spears, bristles, yet how fascinating for our eye to see. (Dr. Edward Degginger Photo)

PLATE 53. "Milkweed." Silky down emerges from the crisp, brittle shell. (Dr. Edward Degginger Photo)

can visually touch the velvet texture of the moth in Plate 38 and feel the contrast with the hard texture of the tree. We feel the softness of the down and the crispness of the pod and seeds in the milkweed (Plate 53). When we look at the thistle in Plate 54 we visually experience the sharpness of thorns.

Visual touching is dependent upon light and the directional movement of light. We see rough or sharp, or smooth or shiny texture in relation to how the surface of planes blocks out or reflects the light.

PLATE 55. "Gray Earth Bowl" by Gertrude and Otto Natzler. The strongly textured crater glaze seems to *be* the bowl. We want to touch it and feel its form. (Courtesy, Syracuse Museum of Art—Ann G. Pass Photo)

A broken surface with many projections can be made to appear more rough by directing light on it from one low source. The dark shadows which the projections cast intensify surface roughness. The same surface may be made to appear relatively smooth by directing on it a diffused light which eliminates shadows. The textural character of a surface is always most apparent at the place where a plane breaks and turns away from the light into shadow. This can be seen clearly on the thistle, the milkweed and the ceramic bowl (Plates 53, 54, 55).

An arranger can modify or intensify the visual sensation of texture by controlling light. Notice in the thistle stalks the greater sense of texture in the half light than in the brightest light. An arranger can create texture by placement of materials. We have seen how a plane can be created by the grouping of shapes into like directional movements. If the shapes are flat, like the leaves in Plate 52, the plane will have the textural characteristics of the material used. If the shapes which make up the plane are three-dimensional, projecting beyond the surface of the plane, a new texture will be created as in the coastal plane of rocks and water, Plate 56, or the Queen Anne's lace (Plate 51).

PLATE 56. "Rocks on the Shore." Individually, each rock is smooth and worn by the sea, but together the rocks form the rough unyielding texture of the shore. (Alicia Parry Photo)

Notice the variety in textural areas in Plate 44. Each material offers a contributing surface of its own, but it is through the grouping of materials into planes that areas of new textural sensation have been created.

Texture is used as a design tool to create rhythm and harmony. However, the greatest contribution of texture to the expressiveness of the arrangement lies in its sensuous, evocative quality.

Hue, Intensity, Value

Without light there would be no color, because *color is light.* We recognize three distinct color qualities in light. These are: *hue,* which refers to spectrum sensation of greenness, redness, blueness and so forth; *intensity* or *chroma,* which refers to the brightness or dullness of the hues, and *value,* which refers to the range from dark to light.

COLOR

As with shape, color qualities change in relation to their relative positions, and also in relation to our distance from them.

Value can be changed by relationships. Darks appear darker and lights lighter when they are placed next to each other. A flower of

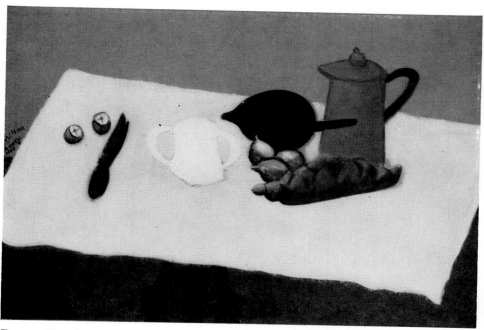

PLATE 57. "Pink Tablecloth" by Milton Avery. Overlapping planes of dark and light create their own space and moving interest in this composition. (Courtesy, Munson-Williams-Proctor Institute—Gift of Mr. and Mrs. Roy R. Neuberger)

light value may look very light when placed next to a dark leaf, but quite dark when next to another flower or leaf of a value lighter than itself. The central flowers in Figure 8a are the same gray but they appear to have different values by contrast with the surrounding values. In the Milton Avery painting (Plate 57) the light appears gray next to the white sugar bowl, but it looks white next to the dark loaf of bread. The black table legs do not appear as black as the black objects on the table because of the surrounding values.

Intensity can be changed by relationship. Colors appear brighter when dull colors or complementary colors are placed next to them, as in Figure 8b. The red in the center of each square is the same red as the sample to the left, but it appears brighter because of surrounding relationships.

Hues are also seen in relationship. We may see a hue simply as yellow until another yellow is placed next to it. Then we may see the first yellow as greenish or reddish, depending upon the quality and quantity of the second yellow, as in Figure 8c.

Color Mixtures—Additive and Subtractive

Countless color sensations can be derived by combining the three color qualities—hue, intensity and value. The mixture may be made directly with light, as by spotlights on a stage, or by blending pigments. The light method is called *additive*, the blending of pigments, *subtractive*, the difference being the way the color qualities are achieved.

We know that white is made up of all the hues in light. When yellow, blue, red, and green light are mixed or *added* together, the result is white. When yellow, blue, red and green pigments are *mixed*, the result is black. This is because pigments selectively absorb or *subtract* hues from light. When all hues are absorbed, we see black. When none is subtracted but all are reflected back to the eye, we see white. When a blue or a red or any other hue is seen, it is because the pigment has subtracted all others and has reflected only the one.

By either method, hue, intensity and value can be changed. I have mentioned that the *primary hues* of light are yellow, blue, red and green. These are called primary because white and all other or *secondary hues* can be made from them. When similar, compatible hues are blended—yellow and red, red and blue, blue and green and green and yellow—intermediate or *analogous* hues are created. Analogous colors are closely-related, neighboring hues, as red, red-purple, purple, or purple-blue, blue, blue-green, and so forth.

Dissimilar, antagonistic hues are called *complementary*. When complementary hues—yellow and blue, red and green, and all corresponding secondary hues, as yellow-red and blue-green—are mixed, the result is not a new hue but a decrease in intensity. If there is more red than green in the mixture, the result will be low-intensity red, if more green, then a dull green. When the mixture is of certain proportions, all hue is lost and we see only gray.

Colors of low intensity are often referred to as *grayed* colors.

Black and white are antagonistic or complementary. The intermediate grays of their blending are *values,* or the degree of lightness or darkness between the two poles of all light and no light. Every blending of light, whether it be additive or subtractive, affects the hue, the intensity and the value of color, depending upon the combinations and amounts used.

Visual Mixture

There is a third way by which colors are mixed—a blending which takes place in the eye.

Scientists have determined that the eye sees color by means of three color nerves which are sensitive to red, blue and yellow-green light. From blendings of these three sensations, we are able to experience all color. The selected color which enters the eye comes from either a pigmentary or a direct light stimulant. The eye must recreate this experience. In doing so, it experiences the color in relation to amount, saturation and position.

If we are forced to look too long at one color, as red, the nerve for red becomes fatigued and automatically switches to the complementary green nerve. Then we see an *after-image* of green. An equal strength of two complementary colors will cause the eye to twitch, to fluctuate back and forth between the two, often with an after-image of gray or yellow. This is frequently experienced with arrangements of poinsettias or red roses.

A green or gray-yellow reverse image is seen in the center of the flower. When the fluctuation is too great, this can be a very uncomfortable sensation.

Analogous colors, when placed in certain relationships, often *visually* mix with their complements. When reds and yellows are placed together, the eye may see not orange, but green in the yellow or blue in the red, thus visually mixing a yellow-green or a red-purple. The center yellows in Figure 8c are visually mixed in that the red-yellow surrounding the one yellow flower makes the flower appear to be more

green. The green-yellow in the second square brings out a complementary red light in the central yellow, making it appear slightly
orange.

Many small points of color are mixed by the eye. Realizing this,
Georges-Pierre Seurat and other early twentieth-century painters de-

PLATE 58. "Fishing Fleet at Port-en-Bessin" by Georges-Pierre Seurat. Pointillism is a technique which can be used in painting, as here, or in mosaic or in arranging. We see everywhere in nature how textures are created and colors visually
mixed by grouping pointlike shapes. (Courtesy, Museum of Modern Art—Lillie
P. Bliss Collection)

veloped a visual-mixture technique known as *pointillism* which we can
plainly see in "Fishing Fleet" (Plate 58). By this method, value, hue
and intensity are modified.

Value can be changed by interspersing dark and light points. The
central square in Figure 9 is of different value from the square on

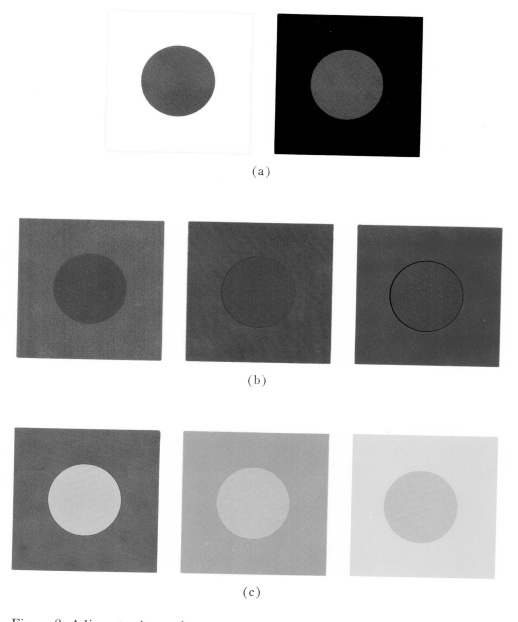

Figure 8. Adjacent color surfaces modify each other: (a) In value, the same gray is used in each square, yet we see the gray disc on the black as lighter in value than the gray disc on the white square. (b) In intensity, the same red is used in each disc, yet we see the intensity as lower when the disc is adjacent to a brighter red surface, and higher when it is adjacent to a red of lower intensity or to a complementary green. (c) In hue, the same yellow is used in each disc, yet one appears more green and the other more orange than the yellow disc surrounded by the neutral gray.

either side of it. Yet it is made up of the same black and the same white as the adjacent squares. The points of black and white have been visually mixed. The central group of berries in the arrangement in Plate 43 contains points of light, as light as the rushes, and dark points, as dark as the table. Yet the overall value of the berries is an intermediate gray.

Analogous hues may be created in the same way. Point groupings of red and yellow flowers like zinnias may give a sensation of orange; or blue and purple delphiniums when grouped in certain relationships will appear intermediate blue-purple.

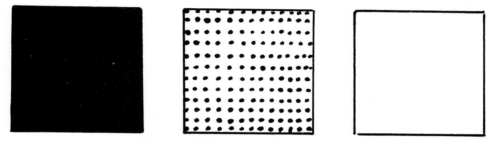

FIG. 9. Pointilistic mixture of color

When points of *complementary* colors are placed so that they will visually mix, the intensity of colors is lowered. A red autumn leaf, dotted with green, will not appear as bright a red as a red leaf with a green border. In the first case, the green has visually mixed with the red and lowered the intensity. In the second, the green edge has made the red center appear brighter by contrast, as in Figure 8b.

No set proportion or rule can be given for visual mixture. When we understand the general way mixtures are created and controlled, we can then experiment and train our eye to sensitivity, see the subtle color variations. Of the three ways in which color can be modified, by additive, subtractive, and visual mixture, the arranger is concerned primarily with visual mixture. Additive mixture of direct light-source should also be considered by the arranger, especially in connection with the staging of exhibition work. Dramatic effects can be created by the use of colored spotlights. Pigmentation mixture does not overly concern the arranger since this is done for her by nature. In this province, it is mostly a matter of training the eye to see and select.

Mood of Color

Color has tremendous emotional appeal. This is so strong that colors are often used to describe our moods as "feeling blue," "seeing red," "in the pink." Color is a strong tool of design and a powerful symbol in the hands of the designer.

We now have the five basic elements of point, line, plane, texture and color. These are the components of all design materials. We cannot, however, proceed with our arrangement until the last basic element—space—has been considered.

Workshop Exercises in Design Analysis of Materials

To get the most out of these exercises, do them searchingly, freely, without a preconceived opinion of what the final form must be. Do not be concerned with rules, judges or prevailing style. Do be concerned with experiencing the abstract nature of your material separately and in a group. These are exercises in learning; the final form may or may not be a flower arrangement, as currently understood.

1. Collect an imaginative variety of point material which can later be used in a three-dimensional construction—berries, flowers, nuts, seeds. Also collect point material for use in a two-dimensional exercise—beads, beans, flower heads, seeds, pebbles, thumb tacks.
2. With the material which is suitable for three-dimensional construction, create a series of arrangements with restricted use of point and color—an arrangement of one like point material; another of the same material but of different sizes; a third with points of different shapes and textures. Create line and plane and space variety by placing and grouping of points.
3. Collect and bring to class for shared experience a variety of line material—corn stalks, flower stems, grape tendrils, roots, twigs, string.
4. Try this series of exercises: Make a construction using only vertical straight lines of one material; another with straight and horizontal lines; one with curved lines of one material; another of curved and straight lines of several materials; another using diagonal and crossing lines or many short lines.
5. Try a series of experiments using like planes, as leaves, or volumetric shapes, as fruit. Vary texture, shape, size and value; use combinations of open and closed shapes; create planes from the grouping of many small shapes.
6. Experiment with combinations of elements as point and line, line and plane.
7. Work out a series of color exercises with torn or cut-paper collage. Color

Aid papers are easy to use. Your designs could have some such color limitations: one with a single hue of varying values and intensities; one of complementary colors of differing values and intensities; one of analogous colors, high intensity, any value.

8. Try a series of collages which begin with a pressed autumn leaf, and then work out a number of color harmonies in relation to it with your Color Aid papers. For example, a red-brown autumn leaf may suggest a collage using only related reds of differing values and intensities, or perhaps low intensity analogous colors or low value complementary greens.

Chapter 4

Reality and Use of Space

Space is the stage on which design performs but every performance is contained in time. *Richard Neutra*

Space is a *real,* a key part of every composition. It must be considered and treated with the same attention as each object placed in it. Space should never be thought of as a "leftover" area, which happens not to be filled by the arrangement, nor as "background," nor as a "void of nothingness." Space should rather be considered and used for what it is—an absolute essential of the life and expressiveness of every design.

There cannot be an arrangement without space. On the other hand, there cannot be a concept of space without objects to delineate it. It is like knowing white through black; no through yes. In experiencing a design, sometimes the space will take on dominant importance, at other times the objects. Between these two optical-emotional pulls, the movements, the energies, the form of the design is created.

The Oriental artist has long been aware of the force and expressive quality of space. He has not hesitated to use it freely in his architecture, painting and also in his flower arrangements. The tradition of Western art has been towards materialism. At times there is such a heaping together of *things* that the space around them is almost obliterated—witness our congested cities!

A consciousness of the importance of space has come slowly, but today more and more architects, city planners, artists and arrangers understand its power and its necessity. A conscious use of space is rapidly becoming one of the dominant characteristics of the art of this century. The Seagram Building in New York (Plate 59) is a prime example of a fine contemporary use of space.

PLATE 59. Segram Building, New York City, by Mies van der Rohe and Associates, Architects. This dignified building, in the confusion of a great city, has created an opening—necessary space of its own and for man's existence. Space moves under the building and into it and is reflected from the sky in the pools and in the walls of glass.

DIMENSIONS OF SPACE

Dimensions are a humanly created method of measuring and evaluating space. Space has only those dimensions which we impose on it or project into it. We must do this in order to find our relationship to space, to have an understandable, manageable area in which to work. The limiting, manmade boundaries immediately give a *frame of reference* against which, and in which, we are able to orient ourselves. A boundary presents a field of space in which to place and relate the elements of a design.

Two-Dimensional Plane

The designer may decide upon a *two-dimensional plane* of space as the working unit, or a *three-dimensional volume* of space. Whichever the choice, the limitations and characteristics of the dimension automatically set the stage for the final form of the design.

The two kinds of space impose quite different designing conditions. The difference should be understood in order to make the best use of the allotted space. Just as limitations of material should be turned to advantage, so should the limitations of space.

The artist, working in two dimensions, uses the boundaries of his chosen plane as a fixed measure. This outer edge is commonly called the *frame of reference*. The inner area or two-dimensional plane, on which the design is created, is referred to as the *picture plane*. The picture plane as well as the frame of reference are constant factors. An artist creates the illusion of three-dimensional space as shapes appear to advance beyond and recede into the picture plane. The equilibrium of this spatial movement is found within the given frame of reference. This is not true with three-dimensional space.

Three-Dimensional Volume

Three-dimensional space is *actual* space, space in which we can physically move. Since there is no constant plane, there can be no constant frame of reference. *We ourselves become the measure of space and equilibrium. We* assume the role of horizontal and vertical axis. Visually we project this axial measure from ourselves to some object which we consider to be in equilibrium—the floor, a wall, a window, a table top, a tree. We then use these projected axes as measures of space and balance. They become our reference areas. In this way, we get a sense of security which gives us freedom to move in various directions without having continually to readjust the objects in space. When a projected ego-centered axis is not to be found, the result is confusion. The trick room that is built with everything leaning or upside-down causes confusion and dizziness because we cannot relate ourselves to the tipsy space.

An artist who works in three-dimensional media, designs not with his eye on a frontal plane, but with his eye on the *back spatial boundary*. This may be an actual boundary such as a wall, or it may be the imaginary wall of the cube of space which the work creates and occupies. The three-dimensional space in which the sculptor and flower arranger work is a *shallow volumetric* space. The artist, dealing with

PLATE 60. "The Arrival in Bethlehem" by Carnelis Massys (Flemish XVI Century). The illusion of great space has here been created by diagonal lines converging to a vanishing point, by a diminishing scale and by a gradual fading of overlapping values. (Courtesy, Metropolitan Museum of Art)

a two-dimensional media, works in a *deep illusionary* space. Compare Plates 60, 61 and 62. In the two paintings, the eye journeys deep, deep into space, but in the sculpture, the eye moves no farther than around, over and into the sculpture.

It is important that arrangers realize the characteristics and qualities of volumetric space and create within its limitations. The arrangement that is related only to a two-dimensional frontal frame of reference, such as a real or imaginary niche, can be nothing but a flat

PLATE 61. "Mountain Landscape with Waterfall." (Chinese, in Sung Dynasty Style, X–XIII Century) Spatial illusion has been created in this brush painting, not by diminishing shapes and converging lines, but by overlapping dark and light shapes and by upward-moving diagonal lines. The distance is as clear and prominent as the foreground. (Courtesy, Metropolitan Museum of Art)

facade. It has not taken advantage of the uniquely expressive characteristics of either two-dimensional or three-dimensional art.

A niche, a room, an outdoor living area is a volume of space. It is in this reality that the arrangement is created. The size of the volume which the arrangement will delineate depends upon the arranger's intent, and also upon other relative design factors in the room, as architectural features and furnishings. With this in mind and heart, we

PLATE 62. "Construction in Red and Black No. 8" by José de Rivera. The space of the sculpture is a shallow volumetric shape contained within and immediately around its created form. (Courtesy, Munson-Williams-Proctor Institute)

generally begin an arrangement by first placing the material so that it will give an indication of the space to be used—height, width and depth (Figure 10).

At the same time, we establish a horizontal and a vertical reference. We must begin a design by making a positive statement about space, and direction in space, but this does not mean that our first statement cannot be changed or modified. The material that was at the outset the tallest, or the widest, or the deepest, frequently is changed as the design plastically progresses. This is especially true of the first directional lines. Because of mechanical difficulties in balancing, the first tall material is often placed much straighter than you will eventually want it to be.

It is a great help when you commence, and throughout the creation of an arrangement, to try to see and feel the larger space-object relationship of the room or other place where the arrangement is to be displayed. This larger space is a field of force which suggests the scale, rhythms, interest and shape of the composition.

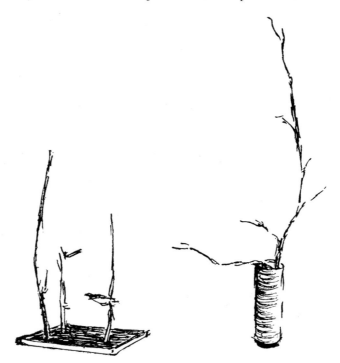

Fig. 10. First placement of material describes the space to be used

Work and Think Around a Composition

As we move about the room, we see the arrangement from changing points in space—higher, lower, closer, farther, from the side or from the front. From every view a good composition holds together in unity and interest.

This does not mean that all sides of a composition must be of equal emphasis. As in some architecture and sculpture, a flower arrangement may, while retaining a total relationship, build up to an "entrance" area, a place of heightened interest. A good composition will always have areas of greater and lesser interest. The eye should, however, be given a means of travel between interest areas, a way to enter *into* and travel *around* the space of the composition from whatever angle it is viewed.

An arranger who thinks and works around a composition is taking advantage of the qualities which three-dimensional space offers. She will develop not only a more stimulating use of space, but will also discover new and imaginative ways of placing materials. For this reason it is helpful to work on a revolving table, as a potter's banding wheel or a Lazy Susan. The arrangement should, however, from time to time be placed on the base or table where it will ultimately be seen, since the height and size of the wheel do influence the design.

ILLUSION OF SPACE

Even though we place material back and front, up and down in actual physical space, we will still experience, along with the knowledge of the actual spatial relationship, an illusionary concept of the space. The optical illusion on which the two-dimensional designer almost solely relies to express space also occurs in three-dimensional designing.

The eye is not a very accurate "seeing machine." It is easily tricked into seeing illusionary shapes and movements, which in turn affect depth perception. A knowledge and controlled use of optical illusion are essential to the artist. Art takes its form and meaning through the imagination. The use of illusion is one of the doors through which we may enter this imaginative world where feeling assumes form, where the invisible becomes visible.

By means of spatial illusion, an arranger can create a world into which we may enter and move and imagine. By value contrast, a large dark leaf may become a deep grotto in an arrangement. By relationship, a twig may look like a great tree, as it often does in Japanese work; notice Plate 26. A light flower can be so placed as to seem to soar into space, as the iris in Plate 63. The tall leafy branch in Plate 64 becomes a tree under which we are invited to move and experience the pleasures and excitements of the arrangement. The eye is invited to move back into the deep shadows under the broad leaves, to climb

PLATE 63. "Spring Iris" by Mrs. Harold D. Warren. Within a three-dimensional area, spacial illusion can be created. In this arrangement an imaginary world of space has been presented through the use of upward-moving diagonal lines, overlapping shapes of dark and light and by relative scale. (Panda Photography)

PLATE 64. "Fall Garden" by Margaret Carrick. Our eye can journey around both the outer and the inner space of this arrangement. The composition creates the space and then lives in the space which it has created. (Jack Carrick Photo)

the side of the pumpkin and to leap upward, forward and back with the light and dark flowers. In both arrangements, space has been animated through the imaginative use of spatial illusions.

Through Color

The color cells in the eye are more quickly stimulated by warm hues —yellow, yellow-red, red-orange. These are called *advancing colors*. Cool green, blue, blue-purple hues recede. Also more intense colors advance because of their greater stimulation, while those of dull, low intensity recede. White and colors of very light value appear to move forward and upward; black and low-value colors seem to move back and downward.

Light values appear larger than dark ones. This makes a difference in the *amount* the designer uses of each. A very small area of warm color will balance a much larger one of cool color. These facts are part of the basic working knowledge of designing.

The illusionary spatial principle we have been discussing could be used in some such arrangement problem as this: A group of dark hosta leaves have created a heavy holelike area in the arrangement. How to correct this? One way would be to introduce enough advancing material into the receding area to bring it back into equilibrium. A bright green leaf, a red or yellow bud or a variegated hosta leaf with specks of white might do the trick. Notice in Plate 65 the use of the light shape in the lower left part of the large dark area. Cover this light shape with your finger and the darks immediately become heavy and "dig" into the canvas.

Another way of countering the dark area in our problem would be to place elsewhere in the arrangement some advancing material of sufficient strength to counterbalance the dark area. The two white flowers in Plate 66 not only help to counterbalance the heavy leaf area, but create a spatial illusion of movement forward and up. Without the white flowers this arrangement would lose much of its three-dimensional spatial quality.

In Plate 64 light has been used to move the eye forward and up from the dark bowl. This is then countered by the dark in the one flower and in the shadows of the leaves under it. The darks help to

PLATE 65. "Blossom" by George Vander Sluis. Space has been animated here by the placement of receding and advancing colors in such a tactile way that we can feel the pulsating growth of the blossoms. (Walter Rosenblum Photo)

carry our eye back into space and down again to the dark bowl. If a light flower were substituted for the one dark flower, the balance of the arrangement would be disturbed, and much of its spatial feeling and imaginative quality would be lost.

Mass arrangements must rely heavily on illusionary space. Without it, they become heavy, uninteresting lumps of materials. There is little actual space left within the mass arrangement in Plate 25, yet the illusion of space is achieved by grouping dark blossoms and leaves next to advancing light flowers. Without the variety and organization of these advancing and receding color values, hues and intensities, this arrangement would be only a confused mass of flowers.

85

Through Texture

Texture also contributes to the illusion of space. Rough textures advance and smooth textures seem to recede into space.

The rough-textured sand to the left in Plate 67 is noticed before the smooth sand to the right of the fence. The level of the sand is the

PLATE 66. "Azaleas" by Rachel E. Carr. Advancing textures, red-lined azaleas and white chrysanthemums, countered by receding darks, have animated the tactile space of this arrangement. (William A. Carr Photo)

same on both sides, yet the textured area appears to be higher and advancing. The textured areas in Picasso's "Rug" (Plate 68) are of the same value as the background, yet they advance almost as much as the white *because of their texture*. Refer again to Plate 64 for the spatial use of texture. The textured white flower appears to be advancing beyond the large smooth pumpkin, and the large smooth leaf at the front moves back into space while the high, rear, textured spray of foliage advances. Both leaf areas are of similar size, shape and value; the spatial contrast is in the texture and related directional movements.

PLATE 67. "Sand Fence." Visually, it is the texturally rich shadow of the fence which holds back the swelling sea of sand. Visual knowledge is always an interpretation of an illusion. (Alicia Parry Photo)

Through Directional Movement, Size and Position

Directional movements and the relative size and position of materials give an illusion of greater or lesser space. Vertical and horizontal lines identify themselves with the human axis. They tend to advance and be more emphatic than the field of space around them. Diagonals, on the other hand, move away from the central axis and give a feeling of a greater depth.

PLATE 68. "Rug" by Pablo Picasso. Overlapping planes of varying textures and values create the ordered space of this design. The sense of transparency, of looking through to another plane, has created a new spatial illusion. (Courtesy, Museum of Modern Art—Gift of Mr. and Mrs. Sam A. Lewisohn)

Each of the paintings in Plates 60, 61 and 65, while using the spatial illusion of color and texture, has created a different illusion of depth through varied use of directional movements, position, and size. The predominantly vertical design in Plate 65 suggests an advancing space. The painting appears to be moving into a space in front of the canvas. Compare this with Plate 60, which creates an illusion of going back beyond the canvas into endless space. This has been accomplished chiefly through the use of converging diagonal lines and a gradual decreasing of size and intensity. The Chinese painting (Plate 61) lies between these two. A sense of distant space has been created through the use of diagonal lines and overlapping planes, yet an advancing movement is maintained by an upward increase in size and repeated emphasis on horizontal and vertical lines.

Now let us consider the flower arranger's use of these principles. We know that the spatial illusion will never be as great as in the paintings because of the physical nature of three-dimensional space. However, we can find the same distinguishing variety of spatial expression in our own medium. Compare Plates 63, 64 and 66 with the paintings. The arrangement in Plate 63, through strong horizontal and vertical emphasis, creates a more shallow frontal space than the arrangement in Plate 64 which uses diagonal emphasis. Here the eye moves diagonally around the lip of the bowl, and from the large frontal leaf back to the smaller leaf, then to a smaller flower, thus creating a deep volume of space. In Plate 66, the dark recessive diagonal is counterbalanced by the advancing movement of the horizontal base and vertical direction of the light flowers.

You will notice in each of these illustrations that either a light or textured area, or an upward moving line has been used near the base of the design. This must be done to bring the design up into space. Shapes placed close to the base plane relate themselves to the horizontal plane, and so often appear heavy and crowded. The same shapes placed near the top of a composition appear much lighter, and the space around them seems larger. Cover the right half of the base in Plate 63, and the arrangement immediately becomes lighter, the space freer. The majority of flowers are balanced high in space with only a tenuous stem-contact with the earth plane.

In nature, observe the difference in spatial feeling between an oak or an elm with wide-spreading branches supported high in space and

PLATE 69. "Magnolia Leaves and Peach Blossoms" by Margaret Carrick. Here light moves into dark and dark into light like folded fingers. This interpenetration of blossoms and leaves creates the animated space of the composition. (Jack Carrick Photo)

a spruce or hemlock with branches sweeping to the ground. Again, it is not a question of one being right and the other wrong, it is a matter of recognizing the spatial difference so that you, the designer, can use and control the various spatial expressions to the greatest advantage in your design.

Through Overlappings

Crossing lines and overlapping planes are ways of obtaining spatial illusion. As we have already seen, the sense of great depth in Plate 61 has been in part created by the overlapping planes of the mountain peaks, each moving back behind another until the greatest depth is reached. In an arrangement, when one stem crosses another, or a leaf or petal overlaps (even though the area between may be physically negligible), an illusion of space is given. This is clearly illustrated by the overlapping magnolia leaves, twigs and blossoms in Plate 69.

Through Fluctuation

And finally an illusion of fluctuation or an oscillating movement, forward and back, back and forward in space, can be created by an interlocking balance between advancing and receding elements in a design. When a proper balance has been reached, as in the ancient yang-yin symbol (Figure 11), it is impossible to say which is the negative and which is the positive element in the design. At first glance, the white seems to dominate a dark field, and then again, the white becomes the space around a dominant dark area. When you look at Plate 61, which do you feel is of greater importance, the mountains or the space around them? At first, the dark receding mountains seem to dominate, but concentrate on the light area, or better still turn the book and study the painting from the side. Then you will see the light spaces move into design prominence.

FIG. 11.   Chinese yang-yin symbol

The arrangement in Plate 69 has created a spatial fluctuation between the interlocking lights and the dark leaf and space areas. Half close your eyes so as to lose detail. Now you will feel the movement back and forth, first the lights are of dominant importance and then the darks.

Fluctuation demonstrates the equal importance of space and objects. We find that space is not a passive container for materials but that it has form and content. Space provides optical forces which are necessary to the life-quality of composition.

Forces of Space

A beautiful tropical fish swimming in an aquarium captures attention so completely that we seldom notice the small eddies, currents and changes in the water as the fish pushes against them. Yet without the resistance of the water, the fish would be unable to move.

The space in which we create our design is just such a resistant force. It is through objects moving with and against this spatial force that life-giving motion is initiated in a composition. An arrangement without movement, like an immobile fish, is visually dead.

All life is movement and constant change. To create is to bring into being new patterns of motion. Once created, the movement must be self-perpetuating. This *is* life, and this is what we mean when we refer to a *living design* or the *life of a design*. Each time we look at an arrangement, to experience it fully, we must be able to recreate the entire composition in our eyes and in our experience. We must move and be moved by the rhythmic patterns of the design. When an arrangement lacks the vital, life-giving spark of movement through spatial forces and tensions, it cannot be recreated. It is dead.

Change in Direction

Crossing lines or any alteration in direction causes an eddy or tension at the point of change. The proof that we feel this tension is demonstrated by our almost uncontrollable urge to soften the force by the use of transitional material. The majority of arrangements in this book have employed some transitional material between changing directional movements. A smooth, unbroken, directional line may create the feeling you wish to express. Realize, however, the value and the force of crossing and changing directional lines. When used properly, they will give vigor and sparkle to your design. The arrangement in Plate 70 has, through the use of crossing lines and directional changes, created a strong spatial tension. The tension is vigorous enough to balance the great weight of the container. Remove the long, horizontal branch on the left, or place the stems behind the handle of the wooden tub, and the composition immediately becomes bottom heavy.

PLATE 70. "Willows in a Rustic Tub" by Rachel E. Carr. The materials and their placement have made space a positive element in this composition. There is the inner and outer space of the tub, the space between the table plane, the handle, and low pussy-willow branches, the space between the line of iris and branches. Each area of space has been animated by varying shape and energies. (William A. Carr Photo)

One of the strongest areas of force in an arrangement is the point where the vertical line of the materials meets the horizontal line of the base.

Sculptors and architects know the importance of introducing a break, such as a line or space, at the base of their sculpture or building. Otherwise, the form seems either to stick or sink into the base plane. Notice how the sculpture in Plate 71 is rounded at the bottom in order to introduce space. The Mies van der Rohe building in Plate 59 appears to be resting on space. Notice how the great columns, the "stilts" which support it, are not camouflaged, but used to visually enhance the design.

PLATE 71. "Two Forms" by Henry Moore. In the sculpture, we can feel the tension in space between the concave and convex forms. We can see that space is not a passive area between solids but a vital factor in the organization and expression of the design. (Courtesy, Museum of Modern Art—Gift of Sir Michael Sadler)

Flower arrangers have been slow to realize that the holding device, the stems, and above all, the space, where stems and container meet, can be expressive parts of a design. The trend has been to fill up the space at the base with a mass of things which gradually blur into the horizontal and firmly attach the arrangement to the table. To remedy this, many arrangers turn to stands and pedestal containers. These do introduce the needed space, but there are other ways. The arrangement in Plate 70 does not hesitate to show the movement of the stems into the base or the water dish in the wooden tub. This un-cluttered openness at the base helps to support the great weight of the prominent container.

The placement of the flowers in Plate 70 also helps to raise the composition up into space. Plates 64 and 66 illustrate a similar plac-ing of value and spatial emphasis high in the design to offset hori-zontal weight. The arrangement in Plate 66 has further lightened the movement upward by introducing space at the horizontal line. Eliminate the small central space in the lowest cluster of leaves and they become uncomfortably heavy and seem to press down on the container.

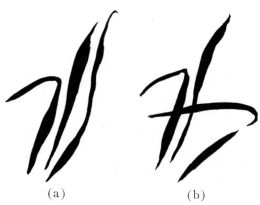

(a)   (b)

Fig. 12.   A different spatial force is felt:
a. When shapes move in one direction.
b. When shapes cross.

The importance of spatial forces as an active factor in the form and life of the design cannot be overemphasized. Indeed the space may assume an importance as great as, or perhaps greater than, the materials. This is true in Plate 70. Compare this arrangement, which has been inspired by an ancient Japanese style, with the contempo-rary sculpture by Henry Moore in Plate 71. It is true the two differ in material and form, but each creates and uses as an integral part of the design strong spatial forces to which the eye and imagination react.

The understanding and controlled use of spatial forces are not matters of period or style but of training the eye to see and experience.

Let us further analyze by diagrams the optic tensions which are created by spatial forces. Let Figure 12a and b represent three grass

blades. In Figure 12a, we are attracted more to the easy vertical movement of the blades than we are to the space around them. The eye
moves easily up and down the lines, but when the lines cross, as in
Figure 12b, we suddenly feel tension, a concentration of force where
the lines cross. The eye now moves back and forth, up and down, between the space enclosures. The lines vie in importance with the space.

Crossed lines are not something to avoid. Only keep in mind, or
in feeling, that their force demands strong balancing pulls. A crossed
line can often bring to life a dead arrangement. We have seen the
interest of crossed lines in nature, Plate 31, and in an arrangement,
Plate 29.

Overlapping

In Figure 12, the crossing lines have made us more aware of
space, first in the illusionary sense of forward and back, and then
by our awareness of space being opened and closed. Space that is
compressed and space that is open differ in expressive force. Notice
the varying forces of the closed space between the handle and tub,
and between the open branches of the willows, Plate 70. The closed
area, even though it is smaller, appears to be the strongest. This is
because of compression.

Compression

In Figure 13, identical branches are placed at the same angle, yet
the visual reaction to each is different. Because of the addition of one
small twig in Figure 13a, and on the side that would seem logically to
need the balance, the branch looks unbalanced and about to fall. What
has happened is that the added twig has compressed an area which,
even though it is smaller than the open area in Figure 13b, seems to
be heavier and more dominant because of the concentration of energies
at each change of direction. The surrounding space is not strong
enough to hold up this "heavy" area. Remove the twig, as in Figure
13b, or lengthen the two left branches so as to provide a larger counterbalancing space-closure and the branch will return to equilibrium.

Closure

Space enclosures, as we have seen, can be created without physically enclosing a space. If a directional path forming an enclosure is

interrupted, the eye will leap across the intervening space in an imaginary line to complete the enclosure, as with the added twig in Figure 13a. Or the eye will complete an enclosure by moving between the terminals of lines.

In each diagram in Figure 13 there is a triangular closure to the right of the branch. It is bounded by the base plane, the diagonal branch and by an invisible line drawn between the terminal ends of these two movements. It is this triangle of space which helps visually to support the branch. Shorten or lengthen the horizontal line to interrupt the size of the closure and the branch falls out of balance.

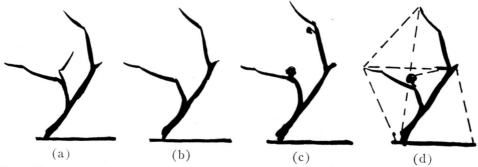

FIG. 13. Spatial forces effect balance. A compressed space (a) is more dominant than an open space (b). Spatial closures between point-objects (c) or between the terminal point-ends of lines (d) are essential to balance.

In counterbalance to this closure are two closures to the left of the branch, the dominant one between the two branches and the subordinate one between the lower branch and the base. Draw the lines between the terminal points of branches and base, and you will have the planes of space which make up the simple branch composition.

We have seen that a closure can be made by the eye moving between tension points. Two blossoms have been added to the branch in Figure 13c, which forms a closure the size of the one in Figure 13a. The visual impact is, however, not the same, since the actual enclosing line in Figure 13a produces a greater force of compression than the invisible line.

In Figure 13d, one blossom has been removed, and a new adjustment of spatial balances immediately takes place. An arranger will find a refreshing variety of interest by creating and using spatial forces in many ways. Observe the emphasis and varied use of space in Plate 72. This composition is particularly interesting in its creation of a large plane of space between the two longest leaves. This large central space visually suspends the arrangement with a kind of sky hook. Cover either of the leaf groups, and the remaining one becomes startlingly disproportionate, and the arrangement sinks into the table plane. Space and its energies are the key to this stimulating composition.

PLATE 72. "Orchids and Driftwood" by Mrs. Fred J. Hay. The space under the curving line of the driftwood and the strong areas of space between the vertical leaves create a lightness which characterizes the expression of this arrangement. (Carolina Studios)

Each opening and closing, crossing and turning in space creates energy. Energy is essential to the life of any work of art. See it, feel it and use it.

WORKSHOP ON SPACE

Here are suggestions to help you develop a sense of space in your arrangements as you work alone:

1. Try to think of space as a real material, not as void.
2. Before you start to work, see or visualize the larger space of the room where the arrangement is to be placed, and think *around* the arrangement.
3. Avoid working in a crowded or cluttered area.
4. Turn the arrangement often as you proceed.
5. Stand back and view your work from various positions and eye levels.
6. Occasionally lift the arrangement so as to silhouette it against a window.
7. As you add each material, check its relationship not only to the other materials, but also to the space created around it. Make sure the space is interesting and well balanced.
8. As an exercise, construct some arrangements with your complete attention focused on space. Use materials which will not require water so that you will be free to place them in any position and from any direction. The end result should be a sculptural construction rather than a traditional arrangement.

Chapter 5

Vision in Motion

The first quality that we demand in our sensations will be order, without which our sensations will be troubled and perplexed, and the other quality will be variety, without which they will not be fully stimulated.
Roger Fry

When you place the first object in space, the life of the design begins, and your eye spontaneously reacts to find an equilibrium between the object, the base plane, and your human axis. Equilibrium—a sense of pause or stability—is necessary to all organisms. But, it must be a changing balance because change is the nature of growth. *Change is life*. In seeing, the eye must have pauses to regenerate the cells of sight and variety to stimulate them to see again. To prove this, stare at one fixed object for a long time, and you will discover that you can no longer see it.

Dynamic Balance

A design with static balance cannot hold our interest. When all objects in the optic field have equal force to attract and repel, they automatically cancel each other and appear dead, as for example, the identical objects on either side of the scale in Figure 14a. In Figure 14b dynamic balance is created by placing the fulcrum or pivot dynamically off center. Equilibrium is then regained by placing at either end by objects of opposing force.

The motion of dynamic balance is generated by inner contradiction. Dynamic balance is a pause between fallings. Two children of the same weight sitting equidistant from the center of a seesaw will be motionless. The rhythm of the game does not begin until one child moves to shift his weight. The child, the "field of energy," on the other end follows suit. Then the seesaw goes up and down in a simple rhythmic line. Before long this one rhythm becomes monotonous and the children are off to a new game, or they introduce innovations to the rhythm. They bump or swing from side to side, or distribute their weight in other ways.

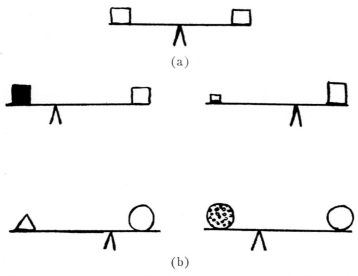

FIG. 14. a. Static equilibrium of like shapes. b. Dynamic equilibrium of unlike shapes.

Interest demands a variety of moving balances. A designer must stimulate eye and mind with changing visual balances. Plants and trees and flowers, which the arranger uses, are not static in nature. There is a constant movement and shifting. Learn this lesson from your materials. Too often you force them into preconceived static patterns.

Symmetry

To achieve dynamic balance, you do not need to avoid symmetry in your compositions, that is, a similarity on each side *in the larger structure*. Subtle rhythms of movement may be created within a predominantly symmetrical framework. The design of the ancient Peruvian embroidery, Plate 73, is symmetrical in its larger structure, but within the simple geometric repeat is an exciting organization. This has been achieved by alternating contrasting lines and values.

PLATE 73. Peruvian Embroidery Fragment (VI Century) A lively rhythmic movement between like shapes of reversed direction and value. (Courtesy, Cooper Union Museum)

PLATE 74. Queen Hat-Shipsut (Thebes, XV Century B.C.) A symmetrical composition with a beautiful balancing rhythm between the detail of the face and the high subtly-curving crown. (Courtesy, Metropolitan Museum of Art)

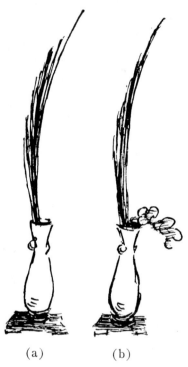

(a)   (b)

FIG. 15. The first movement in
a design creates unbalance (a);
the second, balance (b)

PLATE 75. "Palm Frond and Berries" by
Mrs. Howard S. Kittel. A strong direct balance between vertical, horizontal and diagonal
elements—between the vertical of the light vase
and fronds, the horizontal of the dark table
plane and base and the dark, textural diagonal
of flowers and berries. (Lawrence Joseph
Photo)

Most Egyptian sculpture is symmetrical, yet it is not static. Powerful dynamic forces lie within the form. In the head of the Theban Queen, Hat-Shipsut, Plate 74, vitality is expressed in the movement and relationship between the elegantly detailed face and the tall, subtly curving crown.

In Plate 38 the moth is a vigorous, symmetrical design in nature. The dynamic quality comes from inner variety in the placement and subsequent tensions between the point markings and the texture, color and shape of the wings. *An elemental symmetry is found in most primary natural forms.*

In Plate 25 the arrangement is symmetrical, yet the form is dynamic because of balances and counterbalances within the shape. A basic symmetry can also be seen in the arrangement of Queen Anne's lace, Plate 51.

Asymmetry

Contemporary designers frequently work in *asymmetric* or off-center balance. Arrangers will find greater stimulation if they place the first leaf or flower somewhat off center and slightly out of balance. This will immediately suggest the placing of the next object, which in turn will suggest the next, and so on until a complexity of balances has created the life-form of the arrangement.

Figures 15a and b, based on the arrangement in Plate 75, suggest an out-of-balance, in-balance placement of materials. This immediately establishes the space and the movement of the arrangement.

BALANCE-COUNTERBALANCE

We have seen that symmetrical and asymmetrical designs both achieve a dynamic equilibrium through the principle of balance-counterbalance. This is the method we use in walking. First we throw our weight out of balance as we move one foot forward. Then we recover and again lose equilibrium, as we move the other foot forward, and so on. Balance-counterbalance is the principle of all growth: it is the way in which a design plastically evolves.

Figure 16 illustrates forces that work together and against each other to give dynamic equilibrium. To simplify the example, one large leaf is used in various positions at the right of each diagram. Only the material at the left changes in shape and character.

The length of the horizontal base line is changed to suggest possible container-material relationships.

By *doing,* we learn how to create a rhythm of dynamic equilibrium in our design. By *doing,* we learn what material to select and where to place it in relation to space and other materials. However, we must *feel* the forces opposing each other and must maneuver them in space until our eye is satisfied with the equilibrium.

There is no rule for achieving balance, because each material exerts a different force and demands a different solution. Train your eye to see and to feel and to evaluate, but remember, *evaluation comes only after doing.*

By Opposing Positions

In Figure 16a to e like shapes are put into *motion by change of position and direction.* Beginning with Figure 16a, the position of the leaves creates an up-and-down movement. Because the leaves point in the same direction, there is little pull between them. The greatest tension is between the vertically moving leaves and the horizontal base. Balance lies between these counter pulls. In Figures 16b, c, and d, notice the greater vitality as the leaves pull in opposite directions, until we arrive in Figure 16e at opposing directions which approach horizontal symmetry.

Forces pulling in opposite directions become static when the forces are of equal strength. Movement comes from fluctuating competitive tugs for attention.

By Opposing Points

Figures 16f, g and h illustrate *balanced motion* of the leaf plane *by point.* A point, given a proper amount of space, exerts greater force than a plane. Notice in each diagram the smallness of the point in relation to the size of the leaf and the space required in relation to the position and direction of the leaf. The point in Figure 16f tugs down and to the left to offset the counter movement of the leaf. When the leaf is horizontal and moving to the right, as in Figure 16g, the point must then move high up and to the left in space to counterbalance the downward pull of base and leaf.

(a)   (b)   (c)

(d)   (e)   (f)

(g)   (h)   (i)

(j)

FIG. 16. Dynamic balance is achieved through the counterplacing in space of objects of opposing focal pull by opposing directional movement of like shapes (a–d).

Balance of plane by the tensional pull of point (e–g). Balance of plane by the directional pull of line (h–i). Balance by the pull of opposing sizes and shapes (j–l). Balance of plane by the opposing pull of textures (m–o). Balance through opposing values (p–q).

Figure 16h is just the opposite. In this diagram the point is in league with the base to keep the vertical leaf from shooting out of the space of the design.

Study again Plates 37 and 20. In Rousseau's painting (Plate 37), feel the tremendous pull and stabilizing power of the point moon. In

PLATE 76. "Still Life, 1915" by Henri Matisse. Our vision moves between the fruit and compote on one size of the balance scale, and the downward pull of the napkin on the other. Unconsciously we seek an equilibrium in the space under and around the balancing movement. (Courtesy, Philadelphia Museum of Art—Louise and Walter Arensberg Collection)

the arrangement in Plate 20, see how the point and texture of the flowers exert enough force to counterbalance the intricate basket and the black base plane. In the drawing by Henri Matisse, Plate 76, the point fruit perform almost a magic act in suspending and counterbalancing the draped cloth and the table plane. The tension is so great that the eye is never at rest. This is the life and vitality of the design.

PLATE 77. "The Croquet Match" by Winslow Homer. The relaxed serenity of the figures belies the vital movement of the composition. The balancing rhythm between the lone player, the diagonally moving space around her and the swirl of ladies on the porch is never still. (Courtesy, Mrs. Edwin S. Webster)

By Opposing Lines

Figures 16i and j illustrate *dynamic balance of plane by line.* The force of plane is chiefly that of weight, than of any directional movement which it may have. Even though the leaf planes of the diagrams are strongly directional, they can never have the same directional force as a line. Because of the planes enclosed, compressed space retards the directional movement.

Line is motion. In each diagram the weight and directional motion of the leaf are counterbalanced by the length and directional movement of the line. In Figure 16i the height of the line offsets the horizontal downward pull of leaf, base and spatial closure at the base. The height of the line automatically establishes a large counterbalancing area of space. Compare this with the use of the vertical leaf lines in Plate 72.

In Figure 16j, notice the importance of the slight upturn at the end of the balancing line. If it were removed, the line and the leaf would pull away from each other so violently as to split the design where stems move up from base. In opposing directional movements, there must be a countermovement back in the space of the design, or the design will become static as in Figure 16e, or break in two as did Figure 16j.

In "Croquet Match" (Plate 77) the vertical figure at the right of the painting balances the much larger shape of the grouped figures and the vertical post. Notice how the lone player looks diagonally back to the three figures, who in turn direct the movement forward to the figures on the porch. They are facing, and so returning the movement back to the figure on the right. A moving balance has been created within the frame of the painting.

By Opposing Sizes and Shapes

Figures 16k, l, m illustrate *dynamic balance by opposing sizes and shapes*. Planes and volumetric shapes of various sizes may be used as opposing forces. Their balance is mostly a matter of weight, of finding the correct amount of supporting space.

We must keep in mind that not only actual weight, but also shape-interest of materials exerts a force. Attention is held longer by a shape with interesting contour. If the large shape in Figure 16k were serrated or changed into a more arresting free form, the shape would fall out of balance, *even though size remained the same.*

In Figure 16l, the flower is so large that the leaf has taken on a pointlike quality in relation to it. This is almost a reversal of the balance in Figure 16f. In Figure 16m, we feel the added weight of a volumetric shape. The horizontal line had to be extended to compensate for the added weight of the bell-like flower.

By Opposing Textures

Figures 16n, o, p illustrate *dynamic balance by opposing textures*. Each textural surface exerts a different energy. Therefore, one tex-

PLATE 78. "Thorn Blossom" by Theodore Roszak. A swinging rhythm of line and texture in brazed steel and nickel. (Courtesy, Whitney Museum of American Art)

tured field of energy may be used against another to create dynamic balance. A small amount of high-textured surface generally balances a much larger, smooth, dull surface. If you redraw the textural diagrams and substitute plain for textured surfaces, you will find that equilibrium has been disturbed.

The central textured shape in Theodore Roszak's sculpture (Plate

78) works as counterbalance to the vertical shape at the left. In Plate 64, notice again the force of the textured leaf cluster and flowers as opposed to the smooth textured leaves, bowl and pumpkin.

By Opposing Colors

Each color variation exerts a unique attraction. The dynamic pull will be greatest from opposing complementary hues, as red against green, blue against orange; or from low intensity against high intensity, as dull brown against bright blue, and dark against light.

Warm advancing hues command greater attention than cool recessive hues. Therefore, a relatively small amount of advancing red or yellow will balance a much larger area of recessive blue or green.

As we have seen, white and light values are advancing and appear larger than black areas of like size. Black, however, exerts much greater energy. A small area of dark is capable of balancing a much larger area of white. Figures 16q and u are identical except in value. Figure 16q appears to be falling over to the right, but the dark value in Figure 16r brings the diagram into equilibrium.

In Jean Arp's Constellation (Plate 79), two small black shapes exert energy enough to balance five much larger shapes in dynamic equilibrium. Notice the groupings in space and the tensions between the various free shapes. These shapes could very well be pebbles or any of the natural materials which the arranger uses. Compare the balance through contrasting value used in the paintings in Plates 59 and 77 and the arrangement in Plate 47. Each in its own medium, by the same visual principle, creates that direct statement in space which strong contrasting values produce.

To Feel Balance

To help you experience the force of the tension areas in each of the preceding diagrams more strongly, cover one of the balancing elements. You will find at once that the remaining element appears to be falling. Remove the cover and your eye will be drawn back into a balanced space. This is a good way to check the placement of material in your arrangement. If you cover one element and find that it is missed, you are sure that it is working in your design. If it is not missed, then remove it, or adjust it so that it plays a part, great or small, in the life of the design.

In these diagrams in Figure 16, notice and experience the *variety* in the space movements and their speed. Some rhythms are sharp and staccato, as in Figures 16c and e, others are smooth and even, as in b and j. Some like f and n force us to reach for balance; others like d and g are an easy balance.

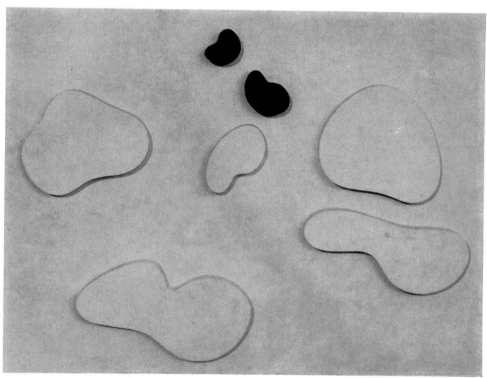

PLATE 79. "Variation I, Constellation with Five White and Two Black Forms" by Jean Arp. Amorphic shapes placed in moving relationship to each other. The two small black shapes animate and balance the rhythms of the larger white shapes. (Courtesy, Munson-Williams-Proctor Institute)

BASIC RHYTHMS

Basic rhythms usually fall into a simple swing, rest, counterswing pattern. The diagrams in Figure 17 suggest some of the rhythms created in the preceding balance diagrams. If further material were added to the diagrams, it would be done in the same balance-counterbalance relationship to the other material, and to the space around it.

Figures 18a and b show the swing, rest, counterswing patterns in

Roszak's welded sculpture, "Thorn Blossom" (Plate 78). Figure 18a represents the larger underlying rhythm which limits the space and sets the basic shape of the sculpture. Figure 18b represents the final enrichment of the basic rhythm. The added swings and counterswings have modified the time, the speed with which our eye moves to the rhythms of the design. They have punctuated and reinforced the basic rhythms but not destroyed them.

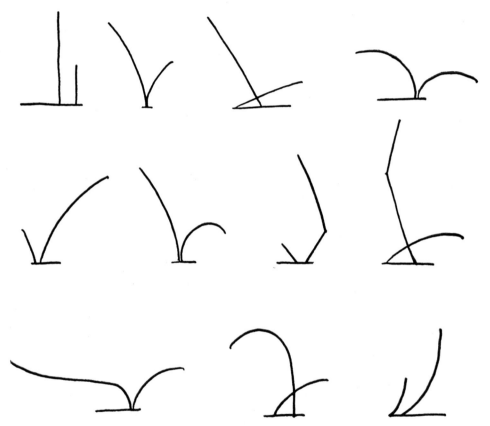

Fig. 17.   Rhythms established by the balances in Figure 16

The moving together of many smaller countermovements into one large rhythmic pattern of swing, rest and counterswing is apparent in all nature. We see it in the rise and fall of waves, in the flight of birds, in the branching of trees, in the relationship of leaf to stem and petal to flower. It is the living pattern of growth and equilibrium.

Relationship of Material to Container

We have demonstrated the role of opposing forces of direction, size, texture, color and shape in creating movement and equilibrium in all design. Each designer must recognize and use the forces of *all* of her material. In flower arranging, the container is one of the materials of the design. As with the others, height, width, color and tex-

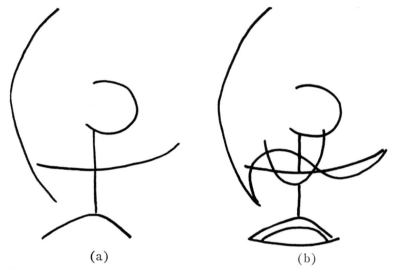

(a)   (b)

Fig. 18. Rhythm is the measured line of motion between balance-counterbalance; it is (a) the main movement of a composition and also (b) the enrichment of it.

ture are forces which must work with and against the material in the design. The container can be brought into dynamic balance by any of the forces or combination of forces which we have discussed.

No predetermined proportion or placement can be given for container-material relationship because each can be infinitely varied. Since antiquity, mathematicians have been fascinated by the prospect of finding a formula for perfect proportion—perfect in that it would please the greatest number of people. In flower arranging, the proportion of one-third two-thirds between container and plant material has been advocated as the perfect proportion. In many cases, this will be the final general proportion. But the discovery and analysis of this come only *after* the arrangement is completed, and then only if you happen to have a mathematical mind.

Figures 19a and b represent two different proportions achieved in identical spherical containers, one by line and one by point. In Figure 19a, greater height is required in the line material to counterbalance the antagonistic pull of the container than is necessary in the related point material in Figure 19b. Yet our sense of equilibrium is satisfied by each diagram. If, however, a pointlike flower or a leaf of varying color or texture were added to Figure 19a and a branch or flower of another color were added to Figure 19b, the proportion of material

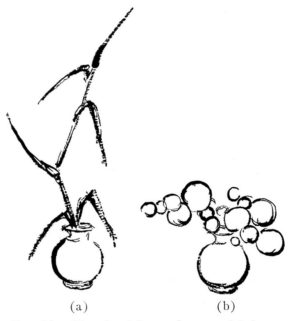

(a)   (b)

Fig. 19.   The visual force of a material determines its proportionate relationship to space, and to container. Its height may be (a) greater than the container or (b) less.

and container would have to be adjusted to a new equilibrium. Also, if containers were changed to dark instead of light, and rough instead of smooth, or if a decoration were added, the proportion would again have to be changed because the containers would then assert a different force. If you place tracing paper over the diagrams and alter the containers, you will feel the change in the design relationships.

Figures 20a and b represent vases of like size and shape, but the relationship of material to them will be different because the vases

(a) (b)

FIG. 20. Containers of the same shape and size may differ in force through color, texture, and applied design.

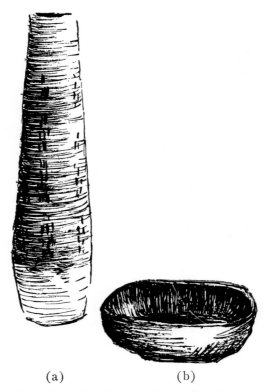

(a) (b)

FIG. 21. The size and shape of each container, will demand a different balancing relationship of plant material.

differ in color, texture, and decoration. Each of these factors will exert a different energy in the life of the design; each will suggest a different choice and placement of materials. For example, one decoration on one container may suggest airy line material, while the dark rough texture of the other may suggest a mass of brilliant flowers or broad-textured leaves.

PLATE 80. "Narcissus in Seika Style" by Rachel E. Carr. At first glance our eye sees only the more obvious side to side rhythm, but look again and again and you will find new measured paths of motion. (William A. Carr Photo)

The shape of the container will suggest, and demand, different combinations of balance. The vertical shape in Figure 21a suggests different possibilities in spatial balance from the horizontal 21b beside it. When you select a container, consider not only size, shape and color but also roughness or smoothness. Be aware of elegance or earthiness, craftsmanship and expressiveness. Approach accessories in the same way, bases, sculpture, wall hangings, or any of the other countless objects which may be used as elements of arranging. Each should be understood as a force in dynamic balance.

Plates 80 and 81 illustrate two beautiful rhythmic balances in space. Each arrangement in its own way invites us to enter into and take part in the creative process of finding relationships and spatial

PLATE 81. "Manzanita Branch and Flower" by Mrs. Howard H. Rawson. A dynamic rhythm occurs between the forceful shapes of the flower, the heavy metal container and the space between the opposing radiating lines, which move to the left and under the container. (Howard H. Rawson Photo)

equilibrium. This is the vitality and living experience offered by good design.

Plate 80, essentially a balance of line and point, creates a positive space of major importance to the composition. (This is diagramed in Figure 22.) The central symmetrically placed space-closure is of such size and importance that we automatically relate it to the horizontal container (Figure 22a). If this were not so, the container

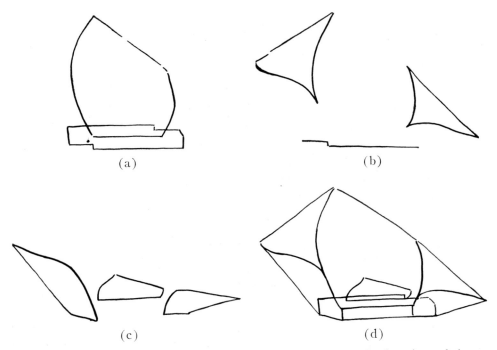

(a)   (b)

(c)   (d)

Fig. 22.   The space within a composition must have an organized variety of shapes and balances.

would be too heavy for the size and delicacy of the flowers. Figure 22b illustrates the major dynamic spatial balance of the composition. Figure 22c points out a secondary movement of transitional space between the horizontal base and the main rhythms of the design. By joining the three diagrams in Figure 22d, we can see the essentially horizontal space which the arrangement circumscribes and animates. Within these major areas the eye will experience many minor rhythms forward and back and from side to side in space.

In Plate 81 each of the methods of achieving dynamic balance, which we explored in the study diagrams, has been employed. The one light, round, textured flower, made even more dominant by contrast with dark glossy leaves, has become the fulcrum of the design balance. By its position, shape, color and texture, this one flower is strong enough to balance-counterbalance all the elements of the design. It is not a static point, but rather one side of a moving scale. We see it as both relating to and acting against the heavy bronze vase, the smooth dark camellia leaves, the textured lines of the branches, and the geometric space of the small stand.

Notice how the stand is related to the design. The progressively enlarged space moving down to the left of the composition from the camellia leaves to the shrub, to the branch, to the stand, is climaxed in the smaller compressed space of the stand. This open volume of space not only supports the great visual weight of container and flower, but also serves as transition between the open space of the arrangement and the closed volumetric space of the container. The line and feel of the manzanita branch relate to the legs of the stand. The character of the stand relates to and is one with the whole composition.

The rhythms of balance-counterbalance are essential to the life of a design, but are not themselves capable of securing the continuance of attention necessary for the integration of the plastic form. The repetition of a simple unchanging rhythm soon becomes monotonous. If the design is to remain vital, the relationship within it must have changing aspects.

Each arrangement which we have analyzed not only has achieved dynamic movement in space, but has also integrated the movements, shapes, colors and textures into orderly patterns of visual experience. Such is the province of composition.

Workshop in Balance and Rhythm

1. In discussion, analyze the balancing rhythms in nature and in the material collected on a field trip.
2. Use this material for a series of balancing exercises: Begin with the dynamic placement of one branch in relation to container and space. Feel free to bend or prune the branch in any way that will increase interest and improve balance.

3. After a variety of balances with one branch, try it with two, then three, and then with more elements—branches, flowers, etc. Work with a variety of containers and bases. Exercises should include all methods diagrammed in this chapter, plus combinations of these methods, as balance of line by plane and texture, volumetric shapes by point and color.
4. Experiment to see how far you can unbalance a shape and still retain a sense of equilibrium.

N.B. In initiating and developing a rhythm, remember to place shapes slightly out of balance. Keep in mind the importance which space plays in balance. Check the space for variety and interest. Monotonous space intervals usually go hand in hand with monotonous rhythm.

Chapter 6

The Form Emerges

The final task of plastic organization is, then, the creation of an optical structure of movement that will dictate the direction and progression of plastic relationships until the experience reaches full integration.

Gyorgy Kepes

Design is the orderly fitting together of visual experiences into an integrated, expressive form. Since design is not a product but a *doing process,* an activity, each designer must arrive at his own design structure. There is no preplanned, correct, compositional structure on which to hang the parts of a design. The way you fit together visual experiences is what creates the structure, but this need not be, and indeed cannot be, by a lone uncharted path of trial and error. We are individuals living in a present culture and we are inheritors of a cultural past. As designers, we are accompanied by a host of fellow artists, those of today and also those who have gone before us.

Study the work of great artists—in various fields of art. Their experience will become your experience. We would be foolish, indeed, if we did not utilize the knowledge of the past and share in the present expression. Every artist has had his master: El Greco learned from Tintoretto, Goya from David, Cézanne from Poussin. Roualt wisely queries, "Have you ever seen anyone born by his own unaided efforts?"

Study the compositional methods and techniques of many artists. Experiment, use the discovered methods in your designs. Make the experience your own and then go on and use it to express your own intent. Mimicry can never create a living, vital art. Growth demands restatement and change.

Approach to Composition

There is no one right way to approach composition, although there surely are many wrong ways. Each artist works according to his own temperament, interests and intent. One arranger may select material and start by placing it intuitively until rhythms and groupings emerge and suggest patterns which can be moved along into a directional structure. This is a kind of "doodling" method which most creative designers use.

Another arranger may begin intellectually with a composition somewhat thought out, and then work toward overall variety and refinement. Whatever the beginning, all compositions must eventually move into a rhythmic, plastic pattern of equilibrium, a balance between the dual forces of what the designer knows and what she feels, between likes and unlikes, motion and rest. The designer must *maintain the vigor* of the visual image *while creating order*—or design. Too much freedom is apt to produce chaotic design; too much intellectualizing may produce static design. A good arranger must have the flexibility to find the balance between these extremes.

We have already considered the ways that movement can be initiated by the spatial placing of material. Our task is now to bind together the rhythmic fields into the larger rhythms of the design. The trip which the eye will take through the design must be carefully plotted and timed by the placement of like-unlike groupings of shapes, directions, colors and textures.

STRUCTURE OF MOVEMENT

As we are drawn from one field of energy to another, the eye is charting a network of lines which weave through the composition. The designer plans these paths so that they will give a stimulating, meaningful journey. Compositional lines move at varying speeds, up and down, from side to side, in and out, on one level and then on another. So it is in music, where the theme will be announced by one instrument and then picked up and repeated by another until a whole musical structure is built.

The final structure of movement or line of an arrangement is like the melodic line which weaves through music. Paul Hindemith in *Craft of Musical Composition* expresses it in this way:

The groups of tones in melody which are harmonically connected are like the links of a chain; they give the melody color and sheen. They are the real body of the melody. It must not be forgotten that a melody is only primarily linear and that the comparison with a curved line applies only to the most obvious, external aspects of a chain of tones. The melodic thread has an ever-changing but ever-present volume of thickness.

Examine Plates 82 and 83. The Martinelli sculpture is a structure of bending, twisting free lines; the Frank Lloyd Wright building is composed of precise geometric lines. Yet both designers have created a medley of varied ever-changing thicknesses, darks and lights, open and closed areas, and counter directions.

PLATE 82. "Demiurge" by Ezio Martinelli. A wildly-moving, expressive composition of free lines in space. (Courtesy, Whitney Museum of American Art)

Line is an inherent part of each way of creating the design structure which we will now discuss. It may be a physical line, a line of continuance, the outline of a plane or an implied line between the tensional pull of like-unlike visual fields. *Motion is the heart of the design.*

Structure Through Likes

There are a number of unifying relationships which the designer may use to create and unite the structure. One of the most powerful is the relationship of likes—like sizes, like shapes, like directions, like colors, like materials.

Each of us in an attempt to find order, looks for familiar objects. In a throng of people in a grandstand, our eye automatically groups people together by the colors they are wearing. The vast audience becomes a fabric of interweaving patterns of dark and light, warm

PLATE 83. A Building in Florida by Frank Lloyd Wright. A structural rhythm of measured geometric lines and changing patterns of light and shadow. (Alicia Parry Photo)

and cool colors. At a meeting or a party, we first seek the faces that are familiar to us, we notice the tall and the short people, men and women. It is a way of orienting ourselves to our environment.

The greatest refinement in seeing is when the individual has trained his eye to abstract the complexity of shapes about him into simple geometric relationships. In Plate 83, it is easy to see the repetitive rectilinear and square shapes which give form to the architecture because

PLATE 84. "Magnolias" by Mrs. DeVere Williamson. A unity in the use of one material with related shapes and colors, and a variety in space and directional movement of line. (Frank Reinhart Photo)

the abstraction has been partly done for us. Also, there is a basic unity of material. This is likewise true of contemporary abstract painting and sculpture. The arranger, while working with the free forms of nature and with a variety of seemingly dissimilar materials, must train her eye to abstract and to see the underlying, unifying similarities.

The arrangement of magnolias in Plate 84 achieves unity through the use of but one material. The flowers *belong* together in nature. Dynamic interest is created by the spatial balance of the branches, the

PLATE 85. "Fruit and Spiraling Line" by Mrs. Howard H. Rawson. The form of this arrangement is created from many interwoven relationships of like and unlike rhythms. This is the task of composition. (Howard H. Rawson Photo)

tension between the various-sized pointlike flowers and buds, and the movement between darks and lights.

The dynamic elements are deftly knit together in an ever-varied line of movement through emphasis of likes. The delicate, glass-stemmed container subtly relates to and intensifies the light elegance of the flowers. Through likes, plant material and container are related. The line of the branch repeats the line of the vase stem. The saucerlike bowl repeats the shape of the open saucerlike flowers. The curved lip of the vase is seen in the curve of the branch, and both container and flowers gradate from dark to light. We also find similarity in the upward movement of petals and buds.

By seeing the *real* abstract quality of the arrangement, we have bundled a complexity of visual sensations into a simple, meaningful,

(a)

Fig. 23. Elements of like focal
pull are organized into unified
movements which become coun-
terparts of the larger design
structure. This may be by a
grouping of (a) like shapes, (b)
like textures, (c) like values.

(b)

(c)

visual experience. As Brancusi has said, "Simplicity is not an end in art, but one arrives at simplicity in spite of oneself, in approaching the real sense of things."

Structure Through Like-Unlike

The arrangement in Plate 85 through the use of seemingly unrelated material has evolved a dynamically integrated form interweaving like-unlike shapes, textures and colors. The largest unifying pattern of likes is in the repetition of circular shapes. Notice in Figure 23a how the major movement of the design is set. This is reinforced and varied by texture in Figure 23b and color in Figure 23c.

Consider that the objects and movements do not have to have an *exact* resemblance in order to relate to each other. They may relate in one grouping through size, in another through color, and in a third through texture. The eye is no respecter of boundaries, but will take any part of an object that will complete a relationship or path of movement.

Observe the variety within each of the movements of likes which have been illustrated. The line in Figure 23a has been animated by differing sizes, weights and spatial groupings. The arrangement is particularly interesting for the balance between the closed round of the fruit and the open round of space, and for the balance between round and textural lines in Figure 23b. In this diagram of like textures, there is a strong counter movement in size and shape. While in Figure 23c, it is easy to see the variety and movements between darks and lights, it is the directed interplay among all these like-unlike movements which creates the structural line of the arrangement.

In Plate 86, the light, point roses are an opposing force to the dark angular lines of pine and the dark vertical container. Yet the roses relate to the clusters of pine needles in shape and size and in their radial construction. The dark, point, rose leaves relate to the needle clusters in shape and to branches and vase in value.

The dynamic placing of likes-unlikes has added zest to the arrangement. A third rose placed high in the composition would have balanced, and certainly would relate to, the other materials, but the arrangement would not be nearly so interesting. A *too even* distribution of exact likes throughout a composition creates an uninteresting

PLATE 87. Iranian Head of Bull (V Century B.C.) The form is created from a stylized rhythmic grouping of lines and textures. (Courtesy, Metropolitan Museum of Art)

PLATE 86. "Roses and Pine" by Mrs. Howard H. Rawson. A dynamic rhythm of line and point, unified by subtle relationships of likes. (Howard H. Rawson Photo)

structure. Seek a stimulating moving harmony through variety in relationships.

In Plate 87, the circular shape of the eye in the fifth-century B.C. sculpture, is repeated, but in different sizes, in the shape of nostrils, in the round stylized lines of hair. The hair texture relates front with side, and then merges into the line which carries the eye along the jaw

PLATE 88. "Madonna and Roses" by Mrs. Howard Oberlin. A simple, quiet composition of deftly handled relationships. (Howard Oberlin Photo)

up the nose and back to the forehead. The curved arc of the nose is repeated in the textured arc of the forehead. The repetitive grouping of lines above the eyes is used in reverse across the nose, and in the textural lines of the hair. With a minimum of interlocking elements, a form of great richness and variety has been created.

PLATE 89. "Christmas Design" by Mrs. William F. Lowry, Jr. A holiday composition, over three feet high, designed for an office building. The bold textures both unify and relate to the large scale of the arrangement. (William F. Lowry, Jr. Photo)

It is always true, a few shapes used well are always worth more than a number used without distinction. Try to achieve maximum interest with relatively few elements. You will find that each arrangement in this book has been created with relatively few of the countless possibilities available to arrangers. Some, as in Plate 49, have limited their design to one shape but of different value and texture; or, as in

PLATE 90. *"Nature Morte au Revolver"* by B. Buffet. The eye follows the bold rhythm of the opposing vertical and horizontal shapes and also reacts to the plastic, spatial control created by the receding dark shapes overlapping the advancing light shapes. (Courtesy, Walter C. Goodman)

Plate 51, to one shape and color. The arrangement in Plate 86 has concentrated on point, line, and value change.

In Plate 88, like point shapes and contrasting values form the main design rhythms. The haloed head of the Madonna relates in value, texture, and shape to the roses. The head becomes part of the vertical line of the rose spray, which, in turn, relates to the vertical line of the figure. The vertical is repeated by the dark leaves. The base relates in shape to the flowers, in value to the leaves.

The arrangement in Plate 89 boldly interrelates *like* strong-textured surfaces with *opposing* directions and values. The outer shape is triangular. It is divided quite evenly by a central axis; yet the design is not static but lively because of the diagonal lines. *The outline of a composition is merely an outer edge which gives little or no indication of the internal plastic forces which create form.*

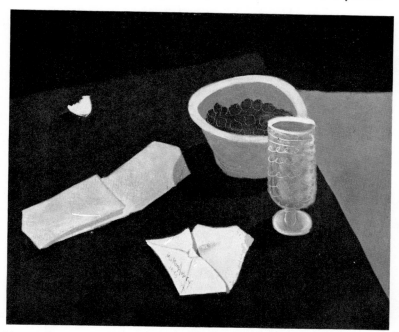

PLATE 91. "Still Life" by Milton Avery. Light objects overlapping a receding dark area weave a controlled rhythm in and out of space. (Courtesy, Philadelphia Museum of Art)

Structure and Depth Through Overlappings

We have seen that an illusion of three-dimensional space or depth can be created by overlapping shapes and that the shapes themselves, which are overlapped and overlap, also have individual qualities of spatial illusion. We have found that each color, texture, size and shape appear to advance or recede, thereby giving the illusion of depth. An arranger can create a structural movement forward and

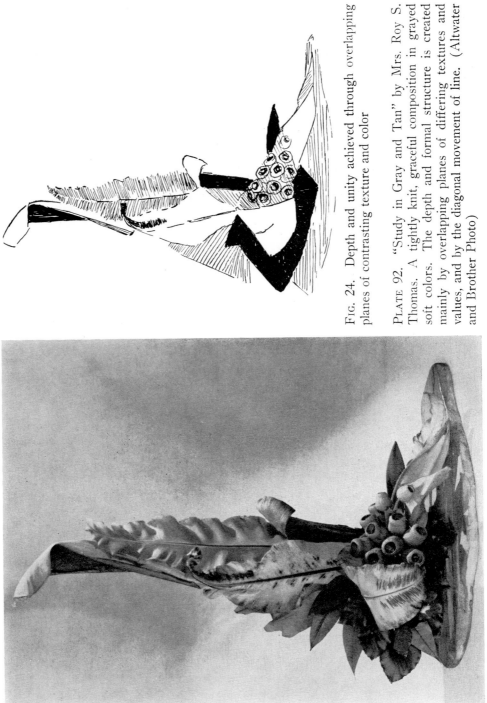

FIG. 24. Depth and unity achieved through overlapping planes of contrasting texture and color

PLATE 92. "Study in Gray and Tan" by Mrs. Roy S. Thomas. A tightly knit, graceful composition in grayed soft colors. The depth and formal structure is created mainly by overlapping planes of differing textures and values, and by the diagonal movement of line. (Altwater and Brother Photo)

back into the space of the composition through the use of overlapping advancing and receding material.

A light area which is moving too far forward in a design can be held back by an overlapping dark shape, as in the painting in Plate 90. Here the light table plane advances from the surrounding gray area. It would float up and out of the painting if it were not held back by the overlapping black objects. Again, we move forward with the white envelope held within the space of the design by the dark barrel of the gun. The reversal is seen in Plate 91 where the dark table plane is brought forward from an even deeper space by overlapping light shapes. The light areas are in turn subtly held back by the overlapping grays of the shadows. In both paintings a sense of depth has been created and controlled by overlapping shapes of varying optical force.

In Plate 92, the arranger has created a sense of three-dimensional space and structural unity by the use of overlapping planes. These major planes have been diagramed in Figure 24. The analysis vividly reveals the spatial movement forward and back in the composition. The interplay between the dark receding areas and the advancing light and textural areas in the lower part of the arrangement is of particular interest. The darks introduce a deep space into the composition, while the overlapping light plane brings the eye forward and up into the vertical movement of the arrangement. The textured plane of seed pods provides a transitional middle space between dark and light. The dominate texture is held in a middle space by the overlapping light leaf. Variations of this forward, back, middle, spatial movement are repeated throughout the composition. *The directional line of a good arrangement has not only height and width, but also depth.*

INTERPENETRATION AND FLUCTUATION

We have seen how a fluctuating, moving space can be created by interpenetrating, intermeshing, opposing elements. Now let us determine how interpenetration and fluctuation can be used to give unity. Figure 25a is a diagram of the arrangement in Plate 69. While the interpenetrating, light, soft points of blossoms and the dark crisp planes of leaves create a spatial fluctuation, they also create the unity of an interlocking, intermediate area between two opposing forces. Figure 25b, a diagram of a Japanese arrangement, illustrates the middle uni-

fying area between interpenetrating light, vertical bamboo canes and
the dark textural plane of foliage.

Notice that the area of interpenetration in each diagram is neither
as light nor as dark as the separate elements, or as smooth or as rough,
or of the same size. A new spatial plane with its own characteristics

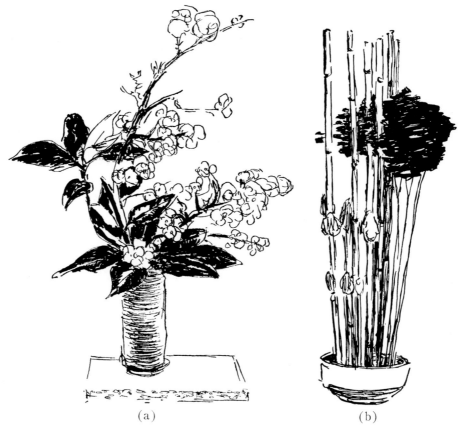

(a)   (b)

FIG. 25.   (a,b) Fluctuation between advancing and receding design elements

has been created. We have a feeling that we are looking through one
plane of space into a deeper space. This method of achieving depth by
looking through a seemingly transparent plane to a plane beyond is
preferred by most contemporary artists to the vanishing-point per-
spective which was developed and used by Renaissance painters. Compare the twentieth-century Picasso rug, Plate 68, which makes use of
interpenetration and a resulting transparency, with the Flemish Ren-

aissance painting in Plate 60. Each has found its own kind of space and unity. Each is expressive of its time.

Three-dimensional design has never been able to suggest such deep space as that in Plate 60. It is foreign to its nature. But it can use the shallow, plastical space of contemporary design. As we become accustomed to seeing and to experiencing space in this way, flower arranging will become increasingly important as a medium of expression.

IMPORTANCE OF LIGHT

Light as color is well used by arrangers, but the use of *direct* light in relation to three-dimensional form is often left to chance. Any artist, working in a three-dimensional medium, is creating light modifiers. Light is turned and bent, intensified and blocked, as objects move into and away from it.

We see three-dimensional form through the changing value of light. *Advancing areas, the areas of highest value face and move toward the direct path of light. Grays are a gradual turning away from light, blacks are a total turning away or blockage from light.* The darkest black will be made by an abrupt turning away from the lightest area.

Form Through Light

In Plate 93, the sculpture can only be seen to advantage with a good light source. The carving is so closely related to the oval shape of the stone that a back lighting or a direct frontal lighting would flatten and lose the form. Light can destroy or intensify three-dimensional form. A designer must always be aware of the source of light, especially when arrangements are exhibited in flower shows.

In Plate 94, the arrangement relies on the modification of light for value interest. The strongest darks have been made by blocking the light. The lightest areas appear where the leaves and sculpture turn into and reflect the light. These are not chance happenings, but an intrinsic aspect of the design structure, carefully developed by the arranger.

Unity Through Light

Light falling on form gives contrast. It can also unify. Many small shapes can be simplified into one plane of light or dark through

PLATE 94. "Duck With Foliage" by Mrs. R. W. Hinz. Reflected light has created unity and sparkling interest in this composition. (Betty Jane Hinz Photo)

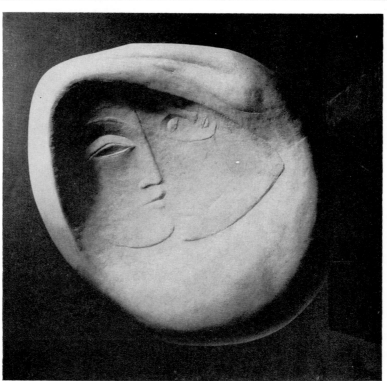

PLATE 93. "Life Form" by Dorothy W. Riester. Without properly directed light, only the outer oval shape of this sculpture could be seen; its form, its inner expressiveness would be lost. Sculpture is a light modifier and depends upon light for form. (Ann G. Pass Photo)

the use of light. Notice in Plate 92 how the many small leaves at the base of the arrangement are unified in the shadow into one simple dark area.

Light reflecting from smooth surfaces will make a unified light value even though the surfaces are of different color value. In Plate 94, the yellow-green pandanus leaves and the brown wood duck become one related plane in the light. Going back to Plate 69, the shiny dark magnolia leaves, which are turned to and reflect the light, relate to the white blossoms in value and not to the surrounding dark leaves. This interchange becomes a part of the interpenetration which is the interesting unity of this arrangement.

Texture Through Light

Texture and color intensity are seen most strongly in middle light. If a texture or color is too strong in one area of a composition, the designer can often remedy this by turning the light away or blocking it from this area. Or he can move the too-strong area directly into the path of the strongest light, and this will reduce the intensity of texture and color. Notice in Plate 93 that the textural marking of the sculptor's tool can only be seen in the middle areas of light, not in the darkest areas or the lightest areas.

COLOR STRUCTURE

We know that colors cannot be experienced as isolated sensations but that they are modified by surrounding colors. The interaction among colors creates powerful forces of energy in the design. Color creates form through these energies and by spatial illusion.

It is important to think of color as a plastic force, not as a quality welded to an object. The shape, size, texture and *color* of an object exert varying tensional pulls. Because of this, any *one* of the materials of an arrangement may enter into a number of separate related movements. For example, the shape may relate a flower to one movement, the color may relate it to another. This overlaying of patterns helps to give structural richness to a design.

If an area in a design is already strong because of position, texture or size, it is often wise to relate the color to a subdued recessive area as has been done with the seed pods in Plate 92. On the other hand, a small unnoticed area can be made dominant by the introduction of a color which strongly contrasts with its environment, as the yellow lemon in Plate 85.

A designer must learn to be selective in the use of color. A well-used limited palette is nearly always more effective than the unrestrained use of many colors. If you study combinations of colors in nature and in fine paintings, you will see how relatively few colors can give the effect of many.

Picasso has said, "In reality one works with few colors, what gives the illusion of many is that they are put in the right place."

LINES OF CONTINUANCE

The law of continuance applies to each movement which we generate in a design. The eye continues, and in the same directional movement, beyond the physical line until redirected by another stimulus. Lines of continuance form powerful, moving bands. These direct and unify the many parts of a design into a final formal expression.

As you compose, follow each movement in continuance. See where the life of the line can be prolonged—by turning the edge of a leaf or the petal of a flower in its directional path. The break in the line and the countermovement are also important. Lines of continuance are an extension and amplification of the rhythmic movements of spatial balance. They should be used to further the dynamic equilibrium of the design.

We have seen in Chapter 3 how lines of continuance form planes or closures in space. The overlapping spatial closures in a design form another unifying, life-giving element.

These overlapping, interlocking closures form a kind of transparent veil of space over and around a composition which sets it apart from all other space. Refer again to Plate 83. Here lines of continuance create a series of overlapping, delineating, spatial planes. Notice in Figure 23a how the overlapping circular planes, created from the directional movement of the fruit and pods, repeat and interlock with the spatial closures of the spiral branch. *The arrangement makes a complete statement in its own world of space.* This is true of all successful design.

In Plate 95, the lines of the sculpture and the form are indistinguishable. The lines, real and imagined, create the textures, the planes,

PLATE 95. St. Elzear of Apt (French XIV Century). A moving rhythm of lines creates the feeling and the unities of this marble sculpture. (Courtesy, Metropolitan Museum of Art)

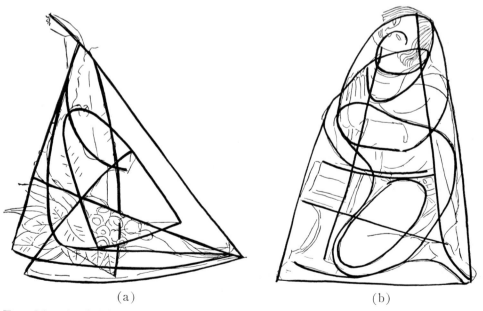

(a)   (b)

FIG. 26. (a,b) Lines of continuance bind together the many separate movements of a design and the space of the design. The varied rhythms of the lines in this design, as in all design, help to communicate the meaning of the composition. It is the same with the gestures of speech or of dance. In fact, the final movement of a design is frequently referred to as its *gesture.*

Figures 26a and b diagram the larger movements of lines and lines of continuance in Plates 92 and 95. The rhythms are expressive of the final gesture of the design. Figure 26a reveals a strong architectural design; the feeling is one of quiet strength. Figure 26b is similar in external shape, yet the rapid, internal rhythms differ in feeling; they are restless and charged with emotion. These are the rhythms which help to communicate the emotion of the sculptor.

MOTION AND REST

To sustain interest and maximum seeing power of the eye, a composition must have both motion and rest. We have seen how the rhythm of a design is created by a series of rests between fallings, as in the motion of walking or the movement of waves. *Areas of heightened interest or tensional pull are necessary to the life of the design.*

These areas of pause emerge as the design evolves. They are an integral part of the rhythms of the design and cannot be added later. Many arrangers develop the habit of placing, as a final touch, an overpoweringly static area usually near the base of the arrangement. This is then called the *focal point*—and indeed it is. It frequently overpowers all other elements of the design.

A good composition should have a number of focal, tensional areas which both momentarily hold the eye and direct it on its journey through the composition. Notice in the El Greco painting, Plate 96, that our eye is arrested not only by the centrally placed child, but also by the other figures, the bowl of fruit, the placing of the hands, the sky, the folds of the robes. Each pause becomes part of a balancing movement which carries our eye to the next pause, and that to the next pause, and so on until our eye has, at varying tempo, encircled the whole design.

The arrangement in Plate 89 has created a focal pause of tensional energy where the vertical material meets the horizontal container. No other accent is needed at this point. The next series of

PLATE 96. "Holy Family" by El Greco. A moving, ever-changing emotional experience develops as our eye lives the dynamic rhythms of line and color. (Courtesy,
Cleveland Museum of Art)

pauses occurs in the point flowers which counterbalance the arresting interests of the central vertical shape.

In Plate 84 a large magnolia has been placed in the center of the composition. However, it is not static. The flower moves into the line of the branch and buds which direct us to the large counterbalancing flower at the extreme left. This in turn is balanced by the flower at the far right of the design. There is no "focal point" in this design, and none is needed.

In Plate 86 the dominant, forceful placing of the central rose has found a counterbalancing, attention-seeking force in the pine branches.

The arrangement in Plate 92 is the only illustration in this book which approaches the flower-arranger's stylistic treatment of one major focal area. If it were not for the strong focal pull of the vertical textured leaf and the top bent leaf, this low focal area would overpower and "freeze" the composition.

In a good design, we should not be conscious of *a* focal point, only of areas of higher and lesser interest, and there should be variety in these interest areas. One may be by position, another by size, another by direction, still another by texture or color.

The element which you choose, the amount and the placement will depend upon the needs of your design and on your imagination. The pauses in motion should create rhythm, not check it. Try to seek this balance.

FINAL INTEGRATION

The *line*, the final formal movement or gesture of a design, is a bundle of integrated, unified, rhythmic movements. In order to understand and control the parts which make up the whole, we have segregated and analyzed the major compositional elements. We can consider the analytical diagrams to be like medical charts used for study of the human body. One chart may be of the nervous system, one of the bone structure, another of the circulatory system. Each is marvelously interesting and intricate in itself. Each *suggests* the human *shape,* but the living human *form* cannot exist until all of the systems are functioning harmoniously.

Figure 23 in this chapter analyzes unified movements through the dynamic placement of shapes, textures, colors and lines. The final form of the arrangement does not emerge until these separate movements are knit into a smoothly functioning, purposeful order. As in the human body, these systems are not created one at a time, but evolve, develop, and grow together until the mature characteristic form is reached.

When an arranger is satisfied that each part of the design is working with every other part to create a form that is pleasing and meaningful to *her,* then the arrangement is completed. Again we state: *Designing is the orderly fitting together of many visual experiences into an integrated, expressive form.*

Workshop in Composition

1. Take a gallery trip to study the compositional methods used in painting and sculpture.
2. Bring art reproduction to class for inspiration and analysis.
3. As a class problem, place tracing paper over a print of a painting or an arrangement. With a pencil, trace the paths of movement in the composition. As you do this, recognize the methods used to initiate and carry along these movements. Is it by color, by texture, a turn of a plane, a point tension, a grouping of likes, a line of continuance? Learn to look for these things in your own compositions.
4. Analyze a group of flower arrangements for abstract shapes, as the repeated circle in Plate 83 or the long elliptical shape in Plate 49. In each composition, look for the *larger* abstract shape—rectangle, triangle, square—which is created by the internal groupings of lines, shapes and space, as was done in the diagrams in this chapter.
5. Create a series of arrangements which are restricted to two contrasting elements. For example, use material which is of the same shape, texture and line, but of contrasting value; another maybe of like shapes and color value but contrasting textures; in another, the shapes might contrast but the elements be alike in all other ways.
6. Experiment with a variety of ways to create tensional areas of interest It may be by position in space, size, texture, color, contrast. Be sure that a single area does not overpower all others to become a "focal point."
7. Experiment with light. Use a movable spot light which can be modified by colored gelatins like those used in stage lighting. Study the changes which

are made on the arrangement both by the direction of the light and by changing color. Observe how texture, color and shape are altered. Notice the important roll of the shadows and the expressive mood quality of the lighting. From your findings work out a series of exercises which will incorporate a specific color light or light from one given direction.

8. Create several arrangements where the shape and the value of the shadows become dominant elements in the composition, and others where a mood is established through lighting, and others where light is used to unify.

$\sim\!\sim\!\sim$ **Chapter 7** $\sim\!\sim\!\sim$

Critical Evaluation

I call a man an artist who creates forms—and I call a man an artisan who imitates forms. *André Malraux*

The creation of an arrangement is personal, yet the arranger must learn to analyze her own work with an impersonal and ruthless eye. This is not a time for rationalizing—"I couldn't get the materials I wanted, there wasn't enough time, this type is not for me"—nor for falling in love with work, because you did it. The design either comes off or it doesn't; it must stand squarely on merit. But take comfort; great artists are almost never completely satisfied with their work.

When you judge your work, first see and experience the whole arrangement. Does it say anything to you? Is it stimulating in its organization, or a static collection of material? Does it hold your interest? Do you have the same, or a heightened experience of pleasure and discovery on a third or fourth viewing as you had on the first? Or does the arrangement seem dead? Do you feel that you have accomplished what you set out to do, and perhaps gained a value on the way?

EXPERIENCE THE WHOLE

If you cannot see and experience your arrangement as a whole, if you are only conscious of individual parts, if you see only to classify and analyze, you have missed the basic purpose of flower arranging. Remember that every art expression is a communication of feeling through form. If the form is not expressive, then the design has failed.

An arranger who does not work with an intuitive or conscious knowledge of the purpose of design, who does not strike the balance between what she knows and what she feels, cannot design creatively or control the direction of her design. An arranger who is working without feeling or knowledge will go on and on aimlessly filling space. Often, since she has no feeling of personal direction, she will seek advice from everyone about her—"What should I use? Where do I place this? Now what do I do? Does it look right?" Or she may copy another arrangement or slavishly follow a set of rules. Then when the result is not all that it should be, she may blame other things but not her own technique, or lack of it.

When "It Doesn't Work"

Creative designing is demanding; it requires selfdiscipline and concentration. At times we all find our attention drifting from the design. We may not catch the break in attention soon enough and find that we have lost control of the design. We are filling space without purpose. We don't know what we are doing or what to do next. If you should find yourself in this dilemma, try some of these ways of extricating yourself.

Reevaluate Material

Think back to your first intuitive feeling about your materials. Ask yourself what was the stimulus? Why did I choose these particular materials? What was my intent at the start? Have I failed to use the unique qualities of my materials? Have I, for example, chosen a branch because of its angular shape and then hidden its contribution among other material?

A reevaluation of materials may help you to see them again. Or it may point out an error in selection. There may be too many things of one texture or value, or there may be a lack of contrast. If your materials were not originally stimulating to you, chances are they will become even less so as the design advances. *The greatest impression is always made on first seeing.* The longer we look at our materials, the less we can see and experience them. While you are working, look away frequently. Look at other shapes and other colors so that you will be better able to see and remain sensitive to the materials in your design.

Remove Material

Is each material contributing and playing its part in the design? If not, remove some of the material or readjust it until it is a working member. When you are dissatisfied with a design and not sure how to improve it, try removing material rather than adding more. Remove material until the force of the design can be felt again. You may take out to the point where everything seems to fall apart. If this occurs and you are forced to make a positive step of correction, then you can be sure you are designing again.

When material is added without your knowing or feeling why, for what purpose in the design, control becomes increasingly hopeless. When the arrangement has reached this state, it is usually wise to make a fresh start. But, first stop a little and do something else to rest your mind. Don't be discouraged. *Twenty spontaneous, joyous tries are better than one labored finality.*

Leave Unfinished Areas

Do you feel uncertain at times as to what to do next? Don't be afraid of this, it happens to everyone. Every artist comes to a point where he doesn't know what to do. When you are not sure, the best advice I can give you is to stop—do nothing more. There are many magnificent paintings still with uncovered areas of canvas because the painter could not decide what to do with them.

It is said that Cézanne had hoped one day to find the solution to a number of unresolved areas in his pictures but never did. To us, such paintings as "Portrait of a Peasant" or "Portrait of Vallier" are complete. Our imagination offers a solution for the uncharted areas and we are the more stimulated for the experience. The eye can deal more imaginatively with space when it is uncluttered than when it is fogged with extraneous fillers and background material.

Hold Up Colors and Shapes

One device which sometimes helps when you are not quite sure what to do next, is to hold up colors and shapes at various points in the design. Sometimes this will produce the needed idea. Also remember to turn the arrangement often (placement on a Lazy Susan helps), and to view it at different distances and from various eye levels. Try changing the source of light. This, too, stimulates fresh seeing and new ideas.

Spot the Problem

Consider also that an area that looks wrong may be the result of a number of not quite-right relationships. It may well be the symptom, the forces of a chain reaction which cannot be corrected until each link is adjusted. Before changing a troublesome spot in any design, look above, below, and across it to the balancing relationships. Feel what is needed in relation to the entire design.

Reconsider Relationships

A problem area can be of value in designing. It stimulates you to find new relationships which you otherwise might not think of. When a design comes to a standstill, it sometimes helps to place a color, a shape, or a line so completely out of balance that the imagination leaps to find some counterbalancing agent. We are forced to reevaluate the importance of each relationship in the design. "Have I made the most of the materials and relationships in my design?" "Could I adjust them to heighten interest without adding other material and other relationships?" "If I add new directional movements, will they clarify the expression of my design, or will they create an entirely new form?"

These are very important questions which each arranger should ask herself as the design evolves. Without this constant check on composition and intent, there is no way of judging what the design should be and when to stop working on it.

When to Stop

Stop when you feel the design has come to life—when it is stimulating and expressive. At this point it may not and probably will not be in perfect balanced relationship. Recall from Chapter 5 that too much unity, a too perfect balance becomes static. Movement is the product of unbalance. The majority of arrangers carry their compositions too far. An unresolved area, a slight unbalance will do away with a stiff formal statement and invite the viewer to enter into the conversation—into the give-and-take of the design. If you feel a combination and placing of materials are exciting, but too bizarre for your present taste, or too unfinished for your sense of design, if you are not quite sure about it, do not continue working on the arrangement. Leave it.

Begin another which may be a development or modification of your idea. This is how a designer grows in experience. An artist's first free sketches are the most valuable part of his artistic growth.

The excitement, the sensitivity, the attitude at the start of a design are all necessary to its final success. So also are the disciplines of composition. Judge your work by first experiencing the whole. *Then* look to the design elements to determine whether any could be adjusted to improve the whole. Check relationships, transitions, movements, pauses, all the contributing parts to the structural motion of the design.

Some Common Design Faults

Here are some common faults for you to consider when checking over your own work:

Bottom Heaviness. Overweight at the base may come about in several ways. There may be a too strong horizontal repetition which holds the eye to the table top. There may be a dominant massing of large or strongly textured or brilliantly colored shapes at the base—a common "focal point" problem.

Too often all open space is excluded from the base. The introduction of even a small amount under a leaf or other material is often enough to give a lightness which will lift the composition above the base plane. Notice in Plate 92 how the introduction of a small air space at the base accomplishes this. Sometimes the base itself can be raised as in Plate 81.

Figure 27 is a drawing of an arrangement that failed because of bottom heaviness. The repetition of the strong texture of the basket by the low flowers, plus the strong shape and color of the jonquils and iris, plus the crowded base massing of interest has made this arrangement unsuccessful.

How can it be improved? Remove some of the base material, or introduce a little space between container and material. Try placing stronger interest, the iris, for example, higher in the design. Figure 27b illustrates some of the changes which can be made to correct the design.

Some of the difficulty in Figure 27a may have been caused by the arranger's desire to hide the holding device. The practice of covering all holders, without regard for the relationship of the added material, is a frequent cause of bottom heaviness. Ivy and broad hosta leaves, tulips with petals spread, rocks and figures are common camouflagers. If you can't think of a way to integrate covering material with the de-

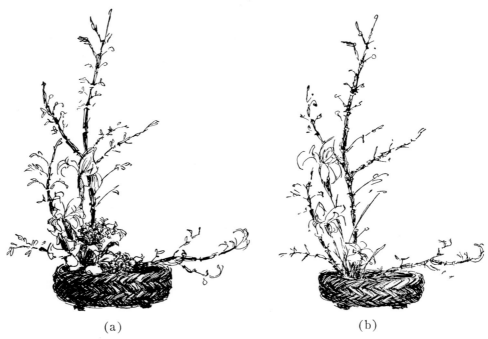

(a)   (b)

FIG. 27. (a) Compositional fault of bottom heaviness, an overconcentration of material at container level. (b) Composition improved by removing lower material.

sign, better leave it out. If the holder is unsightly and does not contribute to the design, try to work out a more skillful mechanics so that there will be no necessity for heavy covering material.

Overstressed Focal Area. We have seen the need for tension areas—areas of momentary pause in the time movement of the design. However, if the focal attraction of an area becomes overpowering, the movement of the design is destroyed. This is a common fault in arranging. In Figure 28 the eye is held to the three center pointlike flowers. Their focal pull is so strong that the rest of the material is reduced to superfluous filling. The arrangement could be improved by grouping, by using material of a different size and tension, and by introducing space. The arrangement in Plate 97, also a mass arrangement, offers a dynamic solution to placing.

In critically judging your own designs, if your eye is held rigidly to one spot, if you are drawn again and again to the same area, you

FIG. 28. Fault of overemphasized focal area

are having "focal point" trouble. You should not be conscious of being held at any area in the design. The techniques of composition should not be labored but appear easy and natural.

Stuffed Space. This occurs when the arranger forgets her intent and is overwhelmed by material. She just can't stop. An arranger who begins with a *preconceived* shape and "line" is usually a space-stuffer. She places her materials not for the lines and shapes which they create, but rather to fill in space.

PLATE 97. "Composition of Spring Flowers" by Mrs. Lawrence Hynes. Light, delicate flowers have not been "held" in composition by an imposing focal area, but rather have *created* a composition of many related focal interests. The form is expressive because each contributing part has been allowed to give its message. (Panda Photography)

Flatness or Lack of Depth

This has already been discussed at great length, but must be mentioned again because it is such a common arranging fault. It is often the result of thinking two-dimensionally, of not turning the arrangement while you work. The movement and spacing in and out, front and back, are extremely important. The interest of light and form depends upon it.

The arrangements in Figures 29 and 31 are both lacking in depth. There is nothing in the front-facing material to lead our eye around the composition, or to help us to imagine or even want to see what the back looks like. There is not an interesting movement or modulation of light in the side which we do see. In Figure 29, if the flowers were of varying sizes or colors and turned at different angles, if they were overlapped by the other material, and if there were more definite organized areas of receding dark, the arrangement would have greater depth.

The front-facing hosta leaves in Figure 31 create a two-dimensional sloping plane of such sharpness that it almost seems that the arrangement has been severed by a sharp knife. The overlapping leaves do tilt the frontal plane backwards, but a forward movement is needed and an open space or diagonal movement around and back. A correction would be to tip the leaf planes forward and backward and eliminate the overpowering focal area.

Figure 28 does not make a good use of space. The shapes almost appear to be made with a cookie cutter. Compare this with the creative use of space and the resulting form and depth in the arrangement in Plate 97.

Monotonous Space Intervals. Sometimes arrangers forget that the space within the arrangement should have as much interest and variety as any other aspect of the design. In some instances, as we have seen in Plate 80, space becomes the dominant aspect.

Figure 29 would be much improved if the monotonous "outline" were broken and space allowed to move into and work with the other elements of the design. Observe in Plate 95 how this has been accomplished. Figure 29 is crowded and confusing. The arrangement in Plate 97, while using as many or even more materials, is airy and inviting.

Unrelated Base or Stand. Figure 30 is a well-designed arrangement except for the base. The base was needed for height, but the shape and character if these scrolls are out of keeping with the cylindrical rough-textured vase and flowers. A block of stone or unpolished wood or a cement block, like that in Plate 69, would be more suitable. A base is as important to an arrangement as a frame to a painting. Too

FIG. 29. Fault of stuffed, poorly con-sidered space

FIG. 30. Fault of relationship of base

often, otherwise successful arrangements are marred by poorly related bases.

The base in Figure 31 is too small and fragile for the massive ar-rangement. In this case the stylistic relationship to the two gazelles is a further detriment. The superior weight and focal prominence of the gazelles further crush the delicate stand.

The base is a part of the total design and Japanese scrolls and rafts are not right in every arrangement.

Poor Choice of Accessories. Accessories should relate to the other materials of the arrangement. Small figures, birds, fish, and animals, glazed ceramic ones in particular, are the great offenders. They are often of inferior design and unrelated in size, color, texture, theme, style or mood. Sometimes accessories are so out of scale with the composition that they vie with, rather than augment, it. This is true of the two gazelles in Figure 31. The figures in themselves are very nice

Fig. 31. Fault of interpretation and relationship of base and accessories

but they are "focal points," competing with the rest of the design. They should be subordinated and drawn back into the composition by an overlapping leaf, or made to look larger by reducing the scale of all the other material.

In Plate 94 the wooden duck could not conceivably be added as an afterthought; it is one with the design. The bird in the James Peale *Still Life* (Plate 98) would be considered an accessory by arrangers. But, is it only an accessory? Is it not a working, integrated part of the design? Perhaps it would be better to abolish the word accessory from our arranging vocabulary and think of every element of our design simply as a material.

The sculptured figure in Plate 99 is the key element of this arrangement. The choice and symmetrical placing of the other elements build up to the climactic expression of the figure.

PLATE 98. "Still Life" by James Peale. Every element in a design is an accessory to that design. In this painting, the fruit, the basket, the bird, the table and the space around them are all accessories to the total form. (Courtesy, Philadelphia Museum of Art)

It must be remembered that the recognizable shape of a figure or an animal or a bird will command more attention than any other element in a design. It must either be allowed to dominate or else be integrated into the composition. Notice how our eye is attracted by the suggested human shape in Plate 89. It has made this piece of gnarled wood more dominate than it otherwise would be.

PLATE 99. "An Altar Shrine for Easter" by Mrs. Philip D. Scott. This is not a composition of materials *with* an accessory figure or a figure *with* accessory materials but a composition. Each element plays its role and is not added as a final "story-telling" device. (Bryan Studio)

Literary Approach. The need to make an interpretive, story-telling arrangement, now so popular, often blinds the arranger to the basic aesthetic contribution which an arrangement can and should make. *Art is not illustration.* It makes the invisible visible, it gives form to feeling. Every element in the design should enter into the expression. The total form of the arrangement *is* the interpretation, *is* the experience of the emotion. In Plate 99, it is not the figure alone which expresses the feeling of the arrangement; it is the sum total of every experience in the design. Th arrangement in Plate 97 interprets a mood, tells a story of spring and romantic loveliness more poignantly than do any of the so prevalent accessory-laden scenes.

The expression of the arrangement begins with the choice of materials and develops as the form emerges. The consciousness of the emotion is the guide to placement, proportion, and accent. It is *total form which communicates* the feeling and tells the story.

Many topical subjects "assigned" to arrangers are not suitable as abstract inspirations, or indeed to the medium of flower arranging. In Figure 31, the design difficulty may have been caused by the arranger's wish to interpret a literal statement, "The Chase." Two gazelles do not make a chase. In creative work, it is well to remember that specific titles, if they are to be used at all, should be given *after* the completion of a work. Not until you have finished a work can you know what the exact interpretation will be. Even then each viewer will have his own, and this is as it should be. The artist creates the experience; the viewer recreates the experience, and interprets it through his own imagination.

Subjective topics are often helpful in stimulating the imagination. The stimulation in interest can be a strong directive in the choice of materials and in design control. This is their value and use in design, not as facts to be illustrated.

Titles which suggest mood, as "Serenity," "Fury"; or a provocative setting, as "Woodland Pool"; or a locale, as "New England," "Rome"; or a season or an element, as "Spring" or "Wind"; or an occasion, as "Birthday Party" or "Easter," are titles which *suggest images* which can be expressed convincingly in the medium of flower arrangement. But such factual titles as "Finish Line," "Rocket to the Moon," "Wheels of Industry," "Fisherman's Haul" are not good because they *suggest things* rather than ideas, and the things which they suggest are often foreign to the intrinsic expressive quality of the arranger's medium. A rocket made of red roses is hardly the best use of flowers.

Poor Transition. An over-emphasized focal area is the most frequent cause of poor transition. It is difficult to move to other areas of the design when one area demands our whole attention. Figure 28 is an example of this common fault. There is a pleasing transition in size, shape, texture, space, and direction from the base to the roses, but no way to move from the roses to the other material. Our eye is trapped in the center.

Figure 30 is an example of a beautifully achieved transition. The eye moves easily from the base of the container to the topmost leaf. It moves from rough to smooth, from heavy to light, from light to dark, in an orderly, interesting progression.

Color Faults. Overemphasis and lack of imagination seem to be the cause of most color faults. By overemphasis, I mean the blatant uncontrolled use of color so that it conceals rather than creates form, and again, the focal emphasis may be overstressed. Color is a powerful element in design; learn to understand and use its force.

Then there is the opposite error: too much concern with blending and the following of formulas which result in milk-toast unimaginativeness. There needs to be more experimenting and less theorizing and a generally more daring approach to color. Don't be afraid to be wrong about color, sometimes to use it badly. Eventually you will develop a rich personal style. This is better than safe "negative good taste." Again we repeat: there is no such thing as a bad color or color combination, it is our ineptness in handling which makes it bad.

Unrelated to Use and Setting. The common fault here is in overstatement, in not distinguishing between an exhibition arrangement and one whose function is to be perhaps only a part of a larger experience as an arrangement at a living room window, or on a coffee table. There are times when a single branch beautifully seen, or a simple placement of three pears in a bowl is all that is required.

Many business establishments, museums, and galleries now use arrangements. These have very special requirements and, in general, arrangers have had only limited experience in working in such extensive space relationships. Too often, compositions are not in keeping with the function and atmosphere of the place. Obviously, the usual competitive flower-show exhibit is not suited to an office or to most business establishments. In galleries and museums also there is too often a sense of competition with rather than a suitability to other objects on display. Compositions for such special settings should not look "arranged," but should be a related part of the larger purpose.

PLATE 100.   Floral Construction for an Art Exhibit by Mrs. William F. Lowry, Jr. This fantasy took its impressive scale and its inspiration from the large space of the gallery and from the spirit of the paintings on display. It was created by and for specific conditions, and could never be seen in the same way and to such advantage in any other environment. This specific importance is understood by all designers who successfully create for specific needs. (William F. Lowry, Jr. Photo)

The twelve-foot composition in Plate 100 was photographed in the Art Gallery of Carnegie Museum. The scale, the choice of materials and the resulting expressive form were inspired by the requirements of the large gallery space, by the flower paintings on exhibit, by the interests and background of the painter.

The large floral construction does not compete with the paintings, but complements them and creates a setting for them. It is not an exhibition piece but rather a part of the spirit of the exhibition. The gallery visitors who know the painter's interest in butterflies immediately understand their significance. To others, they are meaningful in their gallery setting. The butterflies are not accessories, but basic elements in the design.

"That Sculptured Look." In Chapter 1, we discussed the overlapping of the arts. There is an area where arranging and sculpture meet. Not many arrangers work in this marginal region, but for those who do, there are a few pitfalls to be avoided. One is loss of contact with your media. The familiar arrangement category, "the sculptured look," indicates only a certain compactness and strength of form, with perhaps a restrained use of color, nothing more. The arrangements in Plates 89 and 92 are about as sculptured as an arrangement can be and remain an arrangement. *The materials of flower arrangement should not be forced into unnatural positions,* or made to look like something other than what they are. In an arrangement of roses, for example, the roses should not be manipulated into the shape of a boat or a rocket or a figure, but be allowed to express what they best can express in their own way. Often a flower, a curled leaf or a gnarled branch will suggest objects and figures. This can be used to advantage by the arranger, as we have seen in Plate 89, but they should always, as in this arrangement, retain their relationship to nature— that is, if the construction is to remain a flower arrangement.

Mobiles. The moving rhythms of machinery and leaves in the wind have inspired sculptors to create abstract, moving sculpture or mobiles of steel and wire. The flower arranger should, above all artists, find inspiration for these in nature. She should then translate her inspiration into the limitations of her media. Arranger's mobiles and hanging arrangements, should not be poor copies of sculpture, but unique expressions in themselves. Leaves, seed pods, branches, and berries are all mobiles in nature. Seek your inspiration and direction from them. Actually, the limitations of the materials offer a challenge that will help lead to a uniquely expressive form.

PLATE 101. "Spring Iris" by Rachel E. Carr. The materials and techniques of every art make their unique contribution. In flower arranging, it is the marvelous varieties and rhythmic orders of nature. This charming composition of iris in a pool captures and expresses a moment in nature. (William A. Carr Photo)

Lack of Observation

Too often the natural materials of flower arranging are seen only as inanimate colored objects. This is to miss the distinctive beauty of the medium. Allow each material to be itself. Find inspiration from its individual form and from how it grows in nature. The arrangement in Plate 101 has been inspired by the character, by the environment and natural growth habits of iris. It is this which has guided the placements and design organization of the composition, not a manmade dictum of what an arrangement must be. Observation will bring freshness and variety to your compositions and heightened pleasure to you.

Conformity. Conformity is a curse of our time. An uncritical adherance to rules, fear of leaving the security of group thinking, and a lack of adventurous spirit are injecting a kind of sameness into arrangements, as into other art forms. *A creative artist cannot be a conformist.* He must create from his free and inner self. Without the experimenter and the innovator, there would be no progress.

Don't be afraid to make a mistake ; every great work of art has come from a number of wrong tries. Better be wrong now and then and design fresh arrangements that don't always come off, than to follow the crowd and be mediocre.

Are you a slave to your own style? Many arrangers who have received recognition for one type of arrangement are then afraid to try anything new. When you begin repeating your self without saying anything new, you are killing your own creativity, and rigor mortis will soon set in. A creative person never ceases to learn and to grow and to find zest in living. Robert Frost, a truly creative man, has been described as one of the "oldest *living* men today." Conformity has killed more human spirits than has war or disease.

How a Critic Sees and Judges

Now a word about critics. Many artists seriously doubt the value or authority of judges and, in this, unfortunately, they are far too often correct. However, a sensitive critic who does what a critic should do, is of great value to the artist and to the viewing public. Many an artist is totally incapable of evaluating his own work, while the layman is often incapable of experiencing new things *until they are pointed out to him.* Herein lies the province of a critic.

In his book, *Appreciating Painting, Poetry and Prose,* Leo Stein remarks :

Critics are useful for a variety of purposes, but delivering a final judgment is not one of them. A principal role they play is to discover things and bring them to the attention of others. Often their very eccentricities make them particularly sensitive to new and valued expressions. Works of art have to be discovered by someone who will make known what he has found.

A judge must be able to see and experience the form as a whole. He, or among flower arrangers more likely she, will have great sensitivity to design relationships, but will not necessarily have to be an arranger herself. In fact, she may be a better judge if she is not. Arrangers, like artists in other fields, are often prejudiced by their own kind of work.

A judge must constantly be looking for the new and the inventive. By her choice, she should stimulate arrangers to work freely, to experiment and grow. This also works conversely—a critic should also learn and grow by *experiencing* the work of many artists.

In the early years of this century, critics had stultified into academicians. Not until artists broke away from their sterile reign and founded their own unjudged exhibits, did art move forward. Critics and artists today are indebted to these courageous leaders and others like them, for their non-conformity and spirit of adventure.

A critic may specialize in any field of art, but she should be conversant with all the arts, since they complement each other. A wider view develops a discriminating taste, an asset which all judges should have.

The artist or the critic should not, and cannot, judge the worth of a design by a prescribed formula. Each arrangement must stand on its own merit. It must be seen and judged primarily in relation to what it has to say.

A critical evaluation should take account of the degree of success or failure of the formal intent. When the arrangement does not communicate anything but leaves only a feeling of indifference or perhaps confusion, the difficulty can *then* generally be traced to a design fault. It may be a failure in selectiveness, in relationships, in integration. I say *generally* because the critic must know, just as the designer knows, that there is no finality in art. *Art is a relative experience.*

In *Aesthetics and History,* Bernard Berenson clearly sets forth the way to view art critically:

The critic and historian of the work of art, partaking of both the artist's and scholar's activities, should start with being as intuitive towards it, enjoying it as spontaneously and with as little deliberation as its creator who first conceived it. After which only is he called upon to analyse and interpret, to trace and account for its effects, moral and cultural as well as artistic.

Berenson's advice to critics should be heeded by all viewers of art, since an audience acts also as critic and re-creator. This is also good advice to the makers of art—create intuitively, spontaneously, with love. *Then* analyze.

Study of design sharpens perception and selectivity. It stimulates imagination and opens up new fields of experience. It supplies the tools and principles which, when sensitively used, create forms. Through these the artist can speak.

Index